Thank you so much for your support

♡ Eiti

More Than Crumbs

To all of the women who have ever lost themselves trying to find love.

CHAPTER 1

1990

The only memories I have retained from childhood center on my mother, her brother, and her parents. We have always been inseparable. As an only child, I didn't frequently spend time with kids my own age unless I was at school.

My mother worked long hours to support the both of us so I was frequently cared for by my grandmother. While she made dinner for the family, I would stand underneath her in the kitchen. I was always her little helper. In the grocery store I would help pick up items from her shopping list. She would take me back-to-school shopping for the clothing she deemed appropriate for my age. Her and my grandfather had as much of an influence in molding me as my mother did.

My grandmother was a devout Christian who went to church every Sunday morning and returned in the evening for the exact same service. She also attended Bible Study every Tuesday morning and Wednesday evening. I never had a choice of whether or not I would accompany her to these church gatherings. When I wasn't in school or with my mom, I was right by her side.

In church, I would sit in silence and stare up at the stained glass window over the pastor's podium. The image was of the dove carrying a branch in its mouth from the Noah's ark Bible scripture. Every time I looked at it, I wished I could fly away like that dove. My grandmother was diligent about following along with the sermon while highlighting and underlining the corresponding scriptures in her Bible. I had my own little, pink Bible that I would pretend to follow along with whenever she caught me drifting off.

Cheers and affirmations from the congregation would arise as the pastor preached what seemed like the same sermon over and over. Some people would cry, others would clap, and a few would get up and jump around in the aisles. I stayed quiet and observed. Looking around at all of their faces, I would connect them to the stories that I would overhear my grandmother tell.

The man two pews back to the left was the one who couldn't make it home without calling someone to come get him after a night of drinking. The woman across the room in the front was sitting next to the man she started seeing while married to another man. The three older women strategically seated front and center with their extravagant outfits and flashy jewelry were the church's gossip mill. Then there was right hand man of the pastor was soliciting money from the congregation for his own personal 'investment opportunities'.

I couldn't help but wonder why people would pull out their wallets to insert their hard-earned money into an offering plate but they couldn't live by the lessons they praised every week. The offering plate would go around not just once at the beginning of the sermon but again at the end. As a kid I wondered, where was this money going and why was it collected so often? Did Jesus love you more based on how much money you put in?

After each sermon, the pastor would close her Bible and finish her final thoughts. As soon as she was done she was escorted down the center aisle to the back of the church as the congregation rose to their feet and applauded. It was reminiscent of an R&B diva leaving the stage after a concert. Once the doors closed, the hustling assistant pastor would get up to the podium for the closing statements.

On one particular occasion, he suggested everyone pull together a bit more money, separate from their two offerings, to get the pastor a diamond ring to celebrate her decades of service to the church. I thought to myself, that's exactly what she needs to go along with the brand new Jaguar she's driving while some of her congregation is struggling to make ends meet.

The more I saw, the more cynical I became about religion. My focus shouldn't have been on those who surrounded me, I couldn't help but let it negatively influence the message and sanctity the church was supposed to represent. My belief in this higher power of holiness began to diminish as I saw Christians behave the way they did.

The young men and women in my Junior Bible Study group lived a completely different life than I did. Frequently, they would brag about their unmonitored behavior and sexual encounters before our lessons started, putting the scriptures we learned each week to shame. They talked about things I had never heard of and didn't think we should know at that age. One girl shared stories every week about how she let guys do everything but have sexual intercourse so she would remain a virgin.

The adults were no better. They were constantly talking negatively about each other, judging people with different lifestyles than theirs, basing the worth of others on material things, and behaving in ways that were not becoming of Christians. My grandmother on the other hand, diligently led her life by the teachings of the Bible. However, as I grew older, those beliefs weren't ones I could wholeheartedly invest in.

From Pre-K to the 4th grade, I went to a Christian school at the behest of my grandmother. Since Christian school required tuition, my mom would work there a few hours a week doing after-school care, in addition to her full-time job, to offset the cost. It would delight me to see my mom at school, since she worked a lot and I didn't get to spend as much time with her as I wanted.

At school, my teacher saw that I was a fast learner encouraged me to learn how to play musical instruments. I took piano and flute lessons and quickly began to flourish. My mom and grandmother took me to get my little nails done so I could have a piano key design for one of my recitals. I felt very accomplished while up on stage, playing in front of my family and the families of all of the other kids in the school.

I was proud of everything I did at school. That is until one day after class when a teacher's assistant yelled at me in front of my friends for playing games in the middle of the hallway. I took great offense to her embarrassing me in front of other students and thought about a way to get back at her.

One night, my mom and I were sitting around as my grandmother ironed my grandfather's work shirts for the week. I sat there quietly, making sure the story in my head made sense before it came out of my mouth. When there was a pause in the conversation I blurted it out like a battered woman at her breaking point. "One of the women at school hit me on the leg while I was sitting in the hallway."

They both looked at me in shock and asked me to tell them exactly what happened. I claimed that while I was sitting in the hallway talking to another student, this evil old woman loomed over us like a Disney cartoon villain. She snapped at me to move out of the way and before I could get up, she kicked me. Immediately, my mother insisted that she was going to storm into the office and demand this woman be held accountable the very next day.

When I woke up the next morning, I immediately regretted the tall-tale I told to my family. Maybe it was just a dream and no one would bring it up. My mom drove me to school as she normally did and made no mention of the night before. I thought I was off the hook until, instead of dropping me off, she got out and walked me straight into the office to meet with the principal.

We went in to sit down and as I looked out of the window, I saw the woman I had accused of kicking me walk by. Everything else faded into silence and all I could think was, what am I going to say once this woman comes in here? I never thought about what would happen if I had to face her and tell that same made up story.

The principal went back and forth with my mother but at that point, it was like I was watching a silent movie. Once the teacher's aide entered the office, the conversation between the three of them began to fade away. I tuned in just in time to hear my mother say I wouldn't be coming back to the school and then time seemed to stop. What had I done? Was the teacher's aide fired? Did I get myself kicked out of school? Or was my mother so upset about something that never happened that she pulled me out of the school?

Was it too late to say I lied? Even if I did, I'm sure the outcome would've been the same. No one would want a child who would lie about being hit by the staff, especially not at a private Christian school.

My mother led me out of the office and to the parking lot. I looked back and realized how much damage one lie could do. *Years later, with that lie burning a hole in my heart, I confessed to my mom and grandmother that I was never hit by anyone who worked at the school. They both looked at me with confusion, claiming I never told them a story about being hit. The reason I left that school was because they were no longer allowing my mom to work there part-time, and it was too costly without that credit towards my tuition. With that weight lifted off me, I began to question some of the other memories from my childhood.*

After leaving my first Christian school, I ended up at another one closer to home. This school wasn't only an elementary school but also a middle and high school all wrapped in one. On the sign near the main road, you could see where the grades used to stop at 8th but then changed to include all the way up to 12th.

The reason behind the changes were the man who ran the school wanted to keep his daughter and son there as long as he could. The older they got, another grade was added. I was sure if he could, he would build a college campus nearby because his daughter was in the 12th grade when I got there.

The founder of the school was a white, middle-aged man with hair everywhere on his body except for his head. He was extremely menacing and unpleasant to interact with. His teeth were yellow and rotten with large, coarse hands that looked like paws. In each class, there was a demerit system to discipline students.

Each slip of construction paper they used as demerits had a different value. However, the red demerit was like getting the 'straight to jail' card. The worse the offense, the worse each demerit became. Luckily, I kept myself out of trouble so I didn't get sent to his office. If you did, that meant you were there for bad behavior and as a result he would spank the student with a paddle. That's the only time I saw him, when he was walking into his office with his sleeves rolled up, ready to beat the child waiting inside.

One kid in particular, Deacon, would always get red demerits because he was the class clown. The teachers were never fond of his antics. He would always come back from the principal's office with his glasses in his hands, rubbing his red, watering eyes.

My first teacher there was Mr. Carlson. He resembled the hunchback of Notre Dame. He spit every time he talked and he made sure to speak to us as closely as possible. We didn't really learn much because he wasn't great at interacting with children. When he got frustrated we would just make us clean the classroom.

Although it was a Christian school, a lot of the kids knew about a lot of ungodly things. During recess, I would sit with some of the girls from my class while they discussed how they would do things like their bras in order to look older. By that point, I had already grown taller than most of the kids in my class and began to develop a bit; but I listened closely because that was my only exposure to what girls my age were into. Then they would go down the list of all of the curse words they knew. I had to get the words 'damn' and 'ass' in early because they were the only ones I knew.

Being the new girl and the least experienced, I didn't have a lot in common with many of the kids at school. There were only two girls that I got along with. Sonya was a sweet, innocent, and sheltered girl, like me. Then there was Teri, she was a bit rough around the edges and more experienced. She was older than us since she started school late after coming from Puerto Rico. I liked spending time with Teri more, but Sonya was always eager to do things together.

The three of us would spend our recess breaks complaining about class, talking about our crushes who didn't know we existed and taking turns pushing each other on the swing. One afternoon, Teri pushed me on the swing, sending me higher and higher in the air. It was my favorite thing to do because I could close my eyes and pretend like I was flying far, far away from school.

Teri was always better at pushing me, so when she took a break to tie her shoes, I figured I'd stop and wait for her to resume. Instead of taking both of our advice to leave the swing alone, Sonya guaranteed us she could successfully push me the same way. It was against my better judgment to oblige, but I didn't want to seem like I was being mean. Everyone treated her like she didn't know how to do anything right, so I wanted to give her a chance to do this one thing right.

Off I went, soaring into the sky with Sonya as my pilot. At first I thought, this isn't so bad. Then after a few swings, I could feel things going downhill. Well, technically, they began to go to the left. The swing began to wobble instead of going back and forth smoothly. With every swing, I started to get closer and closer to the wooden pole holding the swing set up. I begged for Sonya to stop pushing.

By this time, Teri had tried to resume pushing me, but Sonya wouldn't budge. She was determined to get this right. As I went up, I made my final plea for her to stop pushing me, but it was too late. I flew right into the pole with the entire left side of my body. It felt like I had been thrown into a wall.

I fell off the swing in an indescribable amount of pain and yelled out for help, sounding like a wounded cat. My leg was experiencing such piercing pain and numbness that I didn't think I could move it. I just laid on the ground with my face pressed against the wood chips that covered our playground.

Teri ran over to notify the teachers who were in charge of monitoring students during recess that I needed help. As I slowly lifted my head to look in their direction, I could see them waving me over.

They wanted me to get up off the ground, where I was writhing in pain, and walk over to them. I guess lying face-down in dirt while in the fetal position was just something I did to pass the time during recess. After I didn't move, the aides finally walked over to see what was going on.

I explained what happened and how much pain I was in, and they dismissively told me to spend the rest of my recess sitting in the classroom. After being helped back inside, I sat next to the window trying to imagine myself pre-injury, having fun with the rest of the kids. The isolation felt like a punishment for something that wasn't my fault.

Some of my classmates snuck over to the window to see the damage done to my leg. As kids, their focus wasn't on whether or not I was okay but what the aftermath of my collision looked like. I lifted the skirt of my uniform to reveal a blue and purple bruise the size of a grapefruit on my left thigh. My ankle was also swollen and blue.

The kids began to talk about how much they disliked Sonya and how they should do the same thing to her as payback. I knew Sonya felt bad enough already, but the pain I was in made revenge sound pretty sweet. Eventually the bruise went away and the swelling went down, but my friendship with Sonya never recovered.

On top of that, a few months later Teri's dad was reassigned so she had to move away. From them on, I bounced around from classmate to classmate, making no real connections other than simply having someone to talk to during class. The days of going over to Sonya's house to make friendship bracelets and watch cartoons were over and the afternoons that I cherished soaring on the swing was a thing of the past.

Once it was time for me to attend the 5th grade, my mother and grandparents decided to pull me out of private school altogether. They were displeased with my experiences and decided it was time to give public school a shot. No point in spending money for an institution none of us were happy with. So I found myself once again removed from the friendships I was trying to build and thrust into a brand new school with a brand new way of doing things and brand new people.

When I walked through the door of my new public school I experienced a culture shock. Instead of going to school with kids whose parents paid for them to go to private school, I was thrown into a place where kids attended class because they were required to by state law. There were kids from my side of town as well as ones from other areas I had heard rumors about. Private school didn't prepare me to comfortably interact with kids who hung out all night without supervision, cursed openly, ignored authority, and lived by their own set of rules.

I felt extremely out of place. I had been sheltered at home and in the private schools I attended. My grandmother only allowed me to watch certain TV programs, so I had no guidance on learning what was popular amongst kids my age. The kids in public school spoke a language and exhibited behavior that was unfamiliar to me. I wanted to make friends but didn't really have a common ground to start from.

Through recess and group projects, I slowly began to make acquaintances. The boys in my classes definitely took a liking to me. There was one in particular, Andrew, who stuck out. He was cute and charismatic. We began talking on the phone and spending our lunch breaks together. He was a popular kid and didn't show me a lot of attention at school, which made me try harder.

Our love affair was short-lived, as to be expected during elementary school. I had been dealt the final straw on Valentine's Day. My mom wouldn't allow me to buy him anything for the occasion because according to her I was too young to have a Valentine at all. So I had to get creative in order to not show up empty-handed.

My mother always had an excessive amount of stuffed animals. After narrowing it down to one of the more masculine teddy bears I could find, I stuffed it in my bag and quickly headed to the bus stop. After class, I met up with Andrew and we exchanged gifts. I gave him his gift and he gave me a card that came with two chocolate hearts and a plastic necklace hanging on a yarn chain.

Don't ask me what I was expecting at that age, especially when his gift was a high-jacked teddy bear, but when I saw what he had gotten me, I was unenthused. It was basically a generic drugstore Valentine's Day package he could've given anyone. I shared the chocolates with a couple of kids on the bus and then threw the plastic necklace out of the window as we pulled off from school.

I was already high-maintenance. My family had instilled such love and high expectations for me that it carried over into the rest of my life. That is until a man came into my life who turned everything I thought I knew upside down.

CHAPTER 2

1995

Growing up, my grandfather was the greatest example anyone could ever have of how a man should carry himself and treat other people. He was the head of the household but made us all feel like we were the most important people in the world. My family provided each other with an abundance of care and support. There were only four people in the world I considered family, and what we lacked in numbers we made up in love.

Just after I turned ten years old, my mom sat me down and told me I was going to meet my father. Prior to that moment, I didn't recall ever wondering about him or feeling like someone was missing from my life. His existence seemed to be lost unimportant until that moment. I didn't have an emotional reaction; I wasn't excited or curious. I didn't understand why I had to meet him if he hadn't been around up to that point. Everything seemed to be going fine the way it was.

A few days later, my mother buckled me into the car and I had no idea what to expect. I remember that day like I remember a scene from a movie, as if I was looking at the experience from the outside. My mom told me that my father had been in and out of jail for drug possession, among other things, throughout his life. Those factors played a role in why I had never met him. Now that he was in a pre-release program preparing to get out of jail, she wanted us to meet.

We pulled up to a correctional facility parking lot next to a grassy hill where inmates were doing maintenance on the lawn. After we parked, my mother pointed towards the hill and said, "See that man right there? That's your dad, Jared." As I strained to look through the passenger window of her red Toyota, I followed her finger to a tall, muscular, dark chocolate man who was wearing a white tank top and blue slacks. He looked like he could have been cast as the lead in *The Green Mile*. I was happy that my dad was at least a fit guy, and wondered if I had inherited any of his features.

As we sat, I didn't take my eyes off of that man as I eagerly waited for him to come over. The longer we waited, the more I yearned for him to finish his yard work and so we could meet me for the first time. As I imagined what he would be like in person, I heard my mom talking to someone through the driver's side window.

I looked over and saw a short, heavyset man, whose face was filled with sweat, leaning into the window, smiling at me. As my mother introduced him as my father, I looked back over to the grassy knoll and the man I had been staring at the entire time was gone. I guess when I followed my mother's finger, I missed the portly man working up a sweat she was actually pointing at.

After entering my life that day, he was in and out of it like a tornado over the next few years. He lived with my mom and me for a while after he was released from jail. My mom allowed him to because he needed to have a regular address to report from as a condition of his release. It went from my mom and me doing everything together to having this stranger living in our house, disrupting the life I had grown accustomed to.

He was in no way a good influence on me. He brought people and things around me that I shouldn't have been exposed to. Even worse, I saw my mother truly suffer for the first time because of him. By having him around, I realized 'dad' was just a word. Having a dad in your life wasn't necessarily beneficial if he did more harm than good. He took the smooth, peaceful, and consistent lifestyle I was used to and blew it up.

He couldn't—or wouldn't—maintain an honest living, so he tried to find other ways to make income. There would always be a different vehicle he was driving, a different friend he would bring around, or different merchandise coming through our home. He would even bring home multiple dogs, which I grew to love, until he would abuse and then get rid of them.

I came home one day to multiple holes in the walls of our townhome covered with blood in my mom's room and in the hallway. My mom detailed how Jared had gotten frustrated with our dog, slammed him into the wall and threw him down the stairs to the point where the dog was unconscious. My mom should have seen this incident for the red flag that it was, because that kind of rage against an animal was just the beginning.

He wasn't a man I could look up to or admire; instead, I began to fear him. He weighed over 300 lbs. with a big voice and a very bad temper. I heard a saying once that if your nose sweats that means you're a mean person. His nose would sweat nonstop. My mother tried to shield me from his behavior but when he was upset, he was a force that was too much for her to control.

One Valentine's Day, he was trying to make something up to my mom and gave her a 14K white gold ring with four small diamonds in it. He would always bring things home that didn't come in the original packaging. I don't know if he obtained any of it legally.

Later on he gave me a sweatshirt and a Nintendo game in a plastic grocery bag. I had never played a video game in my life, so the gift choice was rather puzzling. Maybe that was all he could get his hands on at the time.

After several months of arguing, my mom hit her breaking point. She was beyond fed up with his behavior. She realized how much of a negative influence he was on both of us and that he was making no effort to change. While in her bedroom one night she told him to get his things and get out.

Instead of honoring her request, he decided to yell and threaten her. At first, I thought the storm would pass quickly and after exchanging a few choice words, he would go. When the yelling didn't stop, and I heard loud noises from things being thrown around the room, I picked up the dog we had at the time to go upstairs and check on my mom. The dog was a security blanket I hoped would protect me, or at the very least shield me.

As I got to the top of the stairs and looked into her room, I saw him holding her down, screaming at her. While hiding around the corner at the top of the stairs, I asked my mom if she was all right. Jared came to the bedroom door, yelled at me to go back downstairs and slammed the door in my face. At that moment, I didn't know what to do, but I felt like I needed to do something, and fast.

I had never called the police before, but on that night, my father gave me the reason I needed: to protect my mom. In my heart, I believed my mother was in real danger. While I was on the phone, he went on to yell louder and my mother's voice began to sound panicked. I notified the operator that my dad was holding my mom down, yelling, and wouldn't allow her to get up.

The reason he wouldn't leave was because he wanted that

14K white gold ring back, probably to get money for it. He didn't know that my mother had given it to me to wear, and when I realized that's why he wouldn't leave, I was too scared to tell him I had it. I held on to my dog for dear life and waited at our screen door downstairs for help to come.

Once the police arrived, I directed them upstairs. As they began to ascend the stairs, I went outside because I was afraid of what my dad would do to me once he found out I called the cops on him. As my father came down the stairs with the police officers, one of them said to him, "If the lady of the house wants you to leave, you have to go."

As I sat outside, holding my dog tightly next to the bushes in front of our house, people from the neighborhood started to crowd around. They weren't genuinely concerned about us, they just wanted to know what was going on. After one kid asked me what happened, he looked at me and said, "I've never known anyone to call the police on their dad before".

The man who was living with us wasn't so much of a 'dad' as he was a houseguest who had overstayed his welcome. If this were a war, my allegiance was always going to be with my mother. He continued to complain about having to leave as he was gathering his things and walking down the stairs. After the police escorted him out and he finally drove off. He never made an effort to rectify the image I had of him because of that night.

He rarely came around from then on. If he did, it was to try and build a relationship between me and his two sons not between him and me. Unfortunately, they were cut from the same cloth as him. Rough around the edges with no aspirations to be better than what they had seen from the drug dealers and criminals in their neighborhoods. The two of them wanted to be just like their dad, not taking heed that he spent most of his life in and out jail.

Both of them were younger than me, but they undoubtedly had more life experiences than I had. While riding my bike outside, his oldest son, Jared Jr., relayed a message that my 'dad' told me to come in the house. I didn't respect him enough to listen to anything he had to say to me, so I kindly informed him that the man who simply provided the sperm that contributed to my existence wasn't my 'dad'. Of course, he went back and repeated exactly what I said.

Once my mother found out, I got one of the very few beatings I received as a kid and was sent directly to my room. After I called the police to save her from being smothered by him, she chastised me for not considering him my dad. In that instance, she lost a lot of my respect. It was like I stood behind her in a time of battle, but when it came time for her to do the same, she chose to side with the enemy.

One day my mom forced me to spend so-called quality time with Jared and his sons, afterwards we all ended up back at my house. They left the three of us downstairs to watch television together. The thought of watching TV with my half-brothers wasn't my idea of a good time, so I called my best friend and tried to tune out them out.

While on the phone, I noticed my half-brothers staring at me while whispering to each other. I continued to ignore them until they started to move closer. They both quickly got up while the younger one, Nate, began to restrain me against the couch as Jared Jr. climbed on top of me. The phone fell out of my hand but I could hear my friend calling for me, asking what was going on. I started yelling at them to get off me and when that didn't work, I started yelling for help from my mom.

As I was struggling to get free, Jared Jr. began sucking on my neck while Nate continued to hold me down. My body just wasn't strong enough for me to push both of them away so I continued to yell for help, hoping someone would save me from this unbelievably bizarre and uncomfortable situation. This went on for several minutes, and neither of our parents came down to see what was going on.

When they were satisfied with what they had done, they finally let me go. I grabbed the phone, ran into the kitchen, and grabbed a knife from the silverware drawer. It was probably the smallest knife in there, but it was the first one I could get my hands on. I sat in the corner of the kitchen, in the dark, as I informed my friend on the phone what had just happened. She couldn't believe what I told her and advised me to try and get to my room and lock the door.

Jared Jr. came into the kitchen, and I held out the knife between us. I told him if he didn't back away from me, I was going to stab him. I didn't know if I had the strength or ability to do it, but I had to say something to keep him from coming any closer. He mocked me for threatening him with a knife, telling me he had been stabbed before and challenging me to back up my words.

I sat there in silence, hoping he would just leave. The only way I could get to my mom or my room would have been to get past Jared Jr. then rush by Nate in the living room but I was too afraid to do that. As he retreated back into the living room, he insisted they did nothing wrong and I was overreacting. Before he walked away, Jared told me to keep my mouth shut about what they did.

After several minutes of waiting in the kitchen, I felt like it was safe enough to go upstairs and lock myself in my bedroom for the rest of the night. The next morning, I woke up, looked in the mirror, and realized I had received my first hickey. I was speechless and embarrassed. I wasn't using makeup yet, so I didn't have a way to cover it up. It felt like a scarlet letter, as if I had done something wrong. The only thing I could do was wear a scarf to cover it until it went away.

A couple of days later, the marks on my neck slipped my mind when I accompanied my mom to the grocery store. While we were in the vegetable section, she looked at me and asked what was on my neck. I could feel myself getting flushed as it clicked that I didn't wear anything to cover up the hickey. After stalling for a few minutes, she repeated her question. Angrily, I blurted out the story of how I came to receive this eyesore.

I told her I felt let down that she didn't come to help me, or even call out to make sure I was okay. At the time, she thought I was just being loud because we were all playing. She apologized for me being put in that situation. I could tell she was upset, but she didn't say anything else. We never spoke about it again after that, but I gradually saw less and less of my half-brothers, which meant I saw even less of my dad.

There were a few times when he would invite us to his mother's house for good measure. Whenever we would go there I was always surrounded by people I didn't know but were related to. I didn't like going there because every time I did, they all made me feel like I didn't belong. It was a strange feeling to be in a room full of people who were your family and still feel completely isolated, as if you didn't exist.

No matter how many times I went to visit, I never really got to know my dad's side of the family. My mother's and father's families were like night and day. It felt dark, cold, and lonely spending time with my dad's family. My mother's family made me feel safe, loved, welcome, and warm. I rejected the idea that those people related to my dad were even my family. I felt no connection to them.

My father had two brothers, and one of them indirectly had a hand in me being conceived. My mom told me the only reason she started dating Jared was to make his older brother jealous. His brother had one up on him in the looks department, but all three had run-ins with the law and a history of doing time.

Their lifestyles cost the youngest brother his life. Before I was born, he swallowed drugs during a traffic stop to prevent himself from getting arrested. His cousin, who was in the car with him, ran off shortly after the police let them go without seeking medical attention. One of the drug bags ended up bursting inside of him and he died sitting in the car by himself.

As I got older, I saw and spoke to my father less and less. At a certain point, my mother would just tell me he said 'hi' after getting off the phone with him. I rarely spoke to him directly. Every so often, we would come home and there would be some items wedged between our front door and screen door he left for me, still never in their original packaging.

Eventually he just dissipated out of my life. It seemed like I was out of sight and out of his mind. Either my mom stopped telling me about his phone calls or he simply stopped calling altogether.

CHAPTER 3

2000

The private schools I attended from Kindergarten until 4th grade were filled with predominately white students, although there were a handful of minority students in my grade. While watching Saturday morning kids' shows, the main characters were white, so once I got to high school, I felt more comfortable connecting with the white kids.

When I transferred to public school, there were kids of different races and ethnicities from all walks of life. My school bus would drop students off in nice communities with large houses and manufactured lawns as well as the crime-ridden, low-income housing communities. However, I didn't feel like I had anything in common with the black kids from school.

They dressed and spoke differently than I did. The girls were much faster than I was and the guys were sexually aggressive. I didn't feel accepted by them. Whenever I did speak, I would get criticized for 'trying to talk white' or not being black enough.

As I started making friends and hanging out after school, my romantic interests also ended up being white guys. They would range from the alternative guy in the drama club with long hair and spacers in his ears to the white guy with tattoos who only wore wife beaters and hung out with nothing but black guys.

No matter what they were into or what they looked like, there was one thing they had in common: they were horrible choices for me. The guys I was attract to often initiated a gut reaction that screamed 'Back away! Walk, don't run, in the opposite direction!' If they didn't pay me enough attention or the relationship was based entirely on what was convenient for them, I was all-in. I constantly chased guys who were dangling bait that was purposefully out of my reach. The faster I ran to chase them, the further away they seemed to get.

I also had a habit of setting my sights on the most attractive guys or the most popular guys, hoping a relationship would develop. The hardest part was trying to keep the attention of a guy who could easily get attention from every other girl.

My first high school crush was a friend of my neighbor from across the street. His name was Chuck, a tall and lanky white guy with freckles and blondish-red hair. He was a few years older than me, his voice was raspy from smoking, and I found him to be very mysterious. I was drawn to him in an obsessive way.

The fuel of my obsession was that I could never get ahold of him. When I met him, he had no pager or cell phone; the only number I had for him was at his house, but he was never there. I would call all the time (pre-caller ID), hoping he would answer. I could hear the annoyance in his mother's voice every time I called. Eventually, before I could finish my sentence, she would abruptly tell me he wasn't there and hang up.

There was a house down the street from my grandparents' house where he would hang out, so I would frequently walk by to see if he was there. If anyone was outside, I would ask for him and they would always tell me they hadn't seen him. One of my girlfriends, Emilee, was dating my neighbor who introduced us, so she would also set up drive-by dates for us.

After days without hearing from him he would randomly knock on my front door, inviting me across the street. We would have heavy make-out sessions in my neighbor's living room for ten minutes or so, and then he would assure me that I would see him soon. Instead, I wouldn't hear from him for several more days. I felt like an addict.

He would give me just enough to keep me hooked. I would go out looking for him to get that same high again, but could never quite grasp it. Then when he felt like it, he would reappear to give me my fix. It began to drive me crazy. Too crazy for a teenage girl. All of the calling, stalking my neighbor's house, and frequent walks down the street hoping to see him needed to stop.

He was like a ghost. I would hear stories here and there about what he was doing or why I hadn't heard from him from Emilee or her boyfriend. Eventually, I forced myself to give up. I always wondered if he was actually at home, ignoring my phone calls or at the house down the street, hiding from me. He was never around long enough for me to figure that out.

A few months later, I was introduced to a guy named Dennis. He was rough around the edges but had a charming personality. He had pale skin with freckles, short brown hair, and arms full of tattoos. I could tell he was trouble, but it didn't stop me from spending time with him. How different his life was from mine drew me to him more.

Unlike Chuck, he kept in constant contact with me. He would always call me or page me messages while I was in school, and I would call him back as soon as I got home. It didn't take long for him to start sending 17-31707-1 messages which meant 'I love you' in beeper lingo.

Neither of us drove and he didn't go to my high school, so it took a lot of effort to see each other. Sometimes, I would have my mom drop me off at the mall with the rouse that my friends and I were going window shopping. Instead of shopping, we would coordinate with whatever guys we were seeing at the time to meet us there. That was considered our date night.

I was coming into my teenage years, where I found myself getting into certain situations just to try and fit in. I made a friend at school, Ellie, who was an older girl that drove a convertible Mustang and didn't have a curfew. She was beautiful, outgoing, and much more experienced than I was. She took me under her wing and encouraged me to try things I would never dare to do on my own. She lost her virginity at a young age, but since I was still holding on to mine, I sought out tips and advice from her.

She would tell me stories about things she did with guys, but I felt like I was so far away from having those experiences. Even though I was progressively withdrawing from the lessons I had learned growing up in church, I still respected the idea of waiting to have sex. The last thing I wanted to do was be perceived as a slut in high school, which was the label Ellie was working towards.

Luckily, I had another friend, Becky, who was the complete opposite of Ellie, to balance me out. We were both waiting to have sex and connected on things other than boys. We would spend time talking about school, our home life, and our aspirations. Having the two of them as friends allowed me to dabble in being a good girl who followed the rules and also a girl who pushed boundaries and took chances.

After a few months Dennis of talking on the phone a

seeing each other only a handful of times, he suggested I bring a friend to sleep over at his grandparents' ranch. He was also going to invite one of his friends from our school, Eddie. Since Ellie was always down for anything, I knew she would come. I also invited Becky to be my voice of reason in case Ellie got out of control. I lied and told my mom I was spending the night at Becky's in order to get permission to spend the night out.

Becky agreed to drive the three of us the hour and forty-five minutes it took to get to the remote part of Maryland where we were going to stay. Once we arrived, we turned onto a lengthy driveway surrounded by a large lot of land with a ranch-style house at the end and horses walking through the yard. I couldn't believe someone as rugged as Dennis came from such a wholesome upbringing.

As we sat in the car gathering our things, Becky expressed how staying the night worried her. We all promised to look out for each other before getting out of the car. Once inside the house, we were introduced to a tall, dark-skinned, heavyset guy we had never met before, who was not attractive to any of us girls. Ellie took a liking to Eddie and Becky didn't mind hanging out without having a guy to keep her company. While trying to keep up, I agreed to join everyone in the hot tub and partake in a couple of alcoholic beverages.

It didn't take much for me to start feeling loopy from the drink they made me. After a while, Dennis asked me to follow him into a bedroom. Ellie and Eddie followed behind us, leaving Becky by herself with their friend. While Dennis and I laid on the bed, the other two got comfortable on the floor.

It wasn't long before moaning and groaning sounds started coming from the side of the bed. Dennis and I hadn't even gotten out of our bathing suits yet. Since we couldn't drown out the sounds,

Dennis tried to get me to match them. I laid there as he undressed me, kissing all over my body. I contemplated whether or not I should let him go any further.

As we laid naked, making out on the bed, I didn't notice the door open but suddenly, there was a large, dark figure hovering over me. What I was looking at didn't immediately register since I was drunk and Dennis kept pulling my face in to kiss me. While my eyes were close a hand reached out and started touching my neck, moving towards my breasts. I tried to focus my eyes in the dark and yelled out that someone else was touching me.

I don't know if the guys told their friend to wait a few minutes then come in to join whatever was going on, or if he took it upon himself to enter the room. Either way, under no circumstance was I comfortable with him being there and demanded someone get him out of the room. Both guys told him he had to leave and Dennis did his best to calm me down.

I became really nervous and uncomfortable and was hesitant to continue. Up until that point, I had always believed a girl was supposed to lose her virginity to a guy she loved. On top of that, my religious teachings had told me to wait until marriage to have sex.

This wasn't the situation I wanted to be in for my first time. However, with Dennis kissing on my neck and begging to go further, the only thing I could think of was how close he was to the most intimate parts of his body. I wanted to know what it would feel like to listen to the voice inside my own head as opposed to all of the voices from the outside telling me what I should and should not do.

Finally, after much convincing on his part, and me drowning out the fact that two other people were having sex mere inches away from us, I gave Dennis the green light. Before we could get started, Eddie reached out to touch me. I wasn't sure what was going on with these guys but it seemed like they were expecting some sort of orgy.

Eddie touching me was creeping me out, so I swatted his hand away. He retreated back to the floor then he and Ellie went back into the living room. I stopped Dennis to ask him if they were doing these things because they had discussed it before we got there, and he tried to assure me that he didn't agree to or want to share me with anyone. I'm sure he would have said anything at that moment to keep me from changing my mind.

After what seemed like a dozen signs telling me to stop, Dennis put a condom on and did his best to make my first time as painless as possible. At first, there was so much pain but after that subsided, there was an overwhelming sensation of pleasure. It didn't hurt as much as everyone else said it would.

As soon as he turned the lights on, all we saw was a bed full of blood. Whether it was from having sex or my time of the month, the bed looked like a crime scene. Was that a sign from above that I had done something wrong? If it was, there was no turning back—the deed was done. We both showered, changed the sheets, and went to sleep.

Dennis and I saw each other a few times after that, but when he had to move with his family to New York, I heard from him less and less until all communication stopped. Looking back, it wasn't the ideal way of losing my virginity. But once it happened, it opened the door for me to engage in more reckless behavior.

Since I was no longer a virgin, sex wasn't up on a pedestal anymore. It was at eye-level and within my reach. Ellie seemed even more determined to push my boundaries sexually, and I followed her lead. One night, she picked me up and took me to her friend's house.

It was reminiscent of a frat house; they weren't college students, but there were several men living there.

The house was crawling with drugs, alcohol, and women when we arrived. A guy with long, blond hair, ripped jeans, and a t-shirt introduced himself and offered us something to drink. I tried a sip of whatever Ellie had, but it was too strong so I left it to her to finish. Most of the guys were flirtatious, but Ellie came there for one particular guy.

He led Ellie to his room and she brought me with her. Once we got into the room, the lights were off but the TV was on, oddly turned to a children's cartoon. I started to have déjà vu. She and I sat down on the bed as he closed the door. She could tell I was uncomfortable and gave me another sip of her drink to relax.

He told her wanted to go down on her, so she laid back and maneuvered her pants off as I sat right next to her. I didn't know why I was there, so I just kept my eyes glued to the TV. Without saying anything, she tapped my arm and motioned for me to take my pants off. I laid back, stared at the ceiling and did as she told. Ellie leaned over to kiss me and I let her; then entire situation was so bizarre to me that I froze.

I feared that if I left the room, someone else would've probably dragged me into another dark bedroom. She also drove us there, so I was stuck between the guy on his knees and my friend trying to make out with me or risk being stranded.

As Ellie and I were kissing, I felt the guy's facial hair tickling me between my legs. My entire body tensed as he used his tongue on me while his hands worked on Ellie. She continued to kiss me on my lips and neck until she returned her focus to him. This went on for maybe ten minutes until the guy stood up and backed away from the bed. She asked him what was wrong and he explained he couldn't get an erection because of the drugs he was on.

She immediately told me to get dressed and that we were going to leave. I did as she said and followed her to her car, never saying a word. We didn't talk about what happened except for her warning me to stay away from guys who do too many drugs, because they have that problem all of the time.

I took a break from going to anymore strange houses with Ellie. While out with other friends I met a guy at the mall named Josh. A few days later, he invited me over to his house. I told him I was coming with a friend because I didn't want to be there with him alone. My biggest mistake was bringing Ellie, because it was the same as if I had gone alone. She did nothing to keep me from making bad decisions; in fact, she encouraged them and even showed me how.

Shortly after we arrived at Josh's house, he offered us both alcoholic beverages as we sat on the couch. No more than fifteen minutes later, Ellie told me she and his friend were going to walk around outside. I thought that was strange because it was almost winter time and it was freezing that night. As I watched them through his living room window, I saw them head into her car. The next time I glanced outside, her windows were fogged up.

There I was, exactly where I didn't want to be, alone in this guy's house with a buzz. It was clear my friend and his friend were outside having sex, and the look in his eyes implied he expected the same from me. He got me to come upstairs under the guise of showing me his music collection. As soon as we walked through the door he pulled me closer to him, started kissing me, and pushed me down onto his bed.

I didn't feel like I could say no to him. I wasn't even sure if liked him or not, but I came to his house late at night, drank his alcohol, and brought a friend who made it seem like we came there just to have sex. I felt obligated to do what he said. He told me to get undressed, so I did. Before he could see me naked, I climbed under the covers.

He undressed in front of me and got into the bed. When he started touching me, it made me feel disgusting, but I laid there and let him. It was the second time I had ever had sex, but that time didn't feel right. At fifteen, I wasn't mature enough or prepared to make the best choices. I really wasn't mature enough to be having sex at all. I wasn't as respectful of my body as I should've been. Instead of doing things for me, I was doing things that made me feel horrible about myself to please some guy that didn't care about me. Hanging out with someone as loose as Ellie made it seem like it was okay to be loose, as well.

Josh never put on a condom, which I didn't notice at first since I tried to disassociate from my body as soon as I got under the covers. He laid on top of me and began to have sex with me. He didn't notice I wasn't enjoying it, and I'm sure if did notice, he wouldn't care. When he was finished, I felt a warm sensation going through my body and panicked. I yelled at him about why he didn't use protection, and he simply said, "Because it feels better."

I jumped up to rush to the bathroom, taking his entire bedspread with me. I sat on the toilet and prayed for all of his semen to come back out. As I sat there peeing and praying, I began to cry. There I was, having sex with a random guy because I felt like I couldn't object. Not only did I have meaningless, unenjoyable sex with him but he also put me at risk by not using a condom.

Had I been mature enough to make the right decisions, I would've made sure he used protection. Even before getting to that point, I would've said no. Actually, I would never have come to his house that late in the first place, because nothing good was going to come of it. I couldn't speak after I got dressed. I felt dirty, worthless, and beyond disappointed in myself.

What I did wasn't her fault, but I felt disappointed in Ellie, as well. Just because she didn't respect herself enough to keep her legs closed didn't mean I had to be like her. It wasn't worth it to hang out with her if I was going to continue behaving like this.

Without explanation, I stopped hanging out with her altogether. Then I committed to not having sex with anyone else until after I got out of high school. The next time I had sex would be with someone who meant something to me.

The first month of celibacy was easy because I wasn't feeling well. My stomach was upset all the time, I was highly irritable, and all I wanted to do was lie in bed all day. I figured a stomach flu was punishment for my sexual behavior in the past few months. While I was trying to recuperate, my mom agreed to babysit several of her friends' kids. Whenever they came near me, I would bite their heads off. I assumed my hostility was a symptom of not feeling well.

My stomach had been hurting for way too long, so I asked my mom to take me to the health clinic for some medicine. They asked my symptoms, and I told them vomiting, nausea, cramps, and fatigue. After answering all their questions, they drew blood and asked for a urine sample. My mom and I joked around as I sat in the doctor's office, waiting for them to come back with my prescription.

When the doctor walked in holding my file, she looked distressed. She told us, "I have some news. I'm not sure if it's good or not, but you're pregnant." Time stopped. At no point prior to that moment did I ever consider I was pregnant. If I did, I wouldn't have come to the doctor's office with my mom.

I looked over at her and she was frozen. The doctor proudly showed me the piece of paper that measured my hormones and told me I was just a few weeks along. I drowned out everything else she said because from that moment on I wanted to die. Just spontaneously combust right there. I hadn't been sixteen more than two weeks and I was pregnant. What in the hell was I going to do with a baby?

My grandparents were going to disown me when they found out I'd had sex already, and unprotected sex at that. No more sweet, innocent granddaughter treatment. What would people at school think of me? Was my mom going to kick me out? I was in full panic-mode.

The doctor asked me about the particular sexual encounter that led to my pregnancy and after a big swallow, I lied and told them it happened on my first time. "Well how lucky are you!" After a few more routine questions, the doctor told me, "I can see this isn't what you were expecting to hear, but you can make it through this." Once the doctor closed the door, my mom began to question me more regarding every detail about how I got pregnant.

She told me to call the guy that I had slept with as soon as I got home to let him know. Without directly saying it, she told me I had options and to talk with the guy to figure out what I wanted to do moving forward. We held off on telling my grandparents for the time being.

I hadn't even spoken to Josh since the first and only night we spent time together. After sulking around for hours, I paced around my living room as I tried to finish dialing his phone number. Before the last digit, I would hang up. What was I going to say to him? How was he going to react? After dialing all ten digits, I braced myself for the conversation ahead.

When he answered, he sounded surprised to hear from me but gave me a warm greeting. After asking how I was doing, I got straight to the point. "Remember when you didn't use a condom that one time we had sex? Well, now I'm pregnant."

I told him I'd decided to have an abortion and he needed to help with the cost. He was silent for a while and the first thing out of his mouth was, "Are you being serious?" After seriously considering my options, I decided there was no way I could be a teenage mom. I didn't believe I was ready for a child, nor could I give a child the life he or she deserved. Not to mention I would be doing everything alone.

The longer I sat on the phone with Josh, the more sure I was that he wouldn't be there to support me. I didn't want my child to go through life feeling abandoned by their father like I did. Before we got off the phone, I told him I would call him in a few days with more information, and he simply said, "Okay."

Later on, my mom asked how the phone call went and I told her as well as it could've gone. I looked through the yellow pages and called a few places to see how much it would be. Regardless of where I went, it was going to be a few hundred dollars, and from what they told me the procedure was going to be brutal.

When I called Josh back to let him know how much I needed, he didn't answer. I waited for him to call me back, but he never did. Phone call after phone call was unreturned. Day after day, I waited. Finally, I had to tell my mom he wasn't responding. She said a few things under her breath I had never heard her say before.

What was I going to do? My mom made enough to support us, but I didn't want her to have pay for the entire procedure herself. I definitely couldn't ask my grandparents for help because they didn't know I was pregnant in the first place. I was so disappointed in Josh, but I honestly didn't expect any better from him.

The walls were closing in on me. Having an abortion scared me, but having a baby terrified me more. Time was ticking away and I was terrified and desperate, so much so that I even considered throwing myself down the stairs or ingesting poisonous household materials. The longer you waited, the more painful the procedure, and after a certain point, there would be no alternative other than childbirth.

After one last attempt to get Josh to answer the phone, I left him a vile voicemail then cried alone in my room for hours. My mind raced what I was going to do, and I considered what would happen if I started taking birth control pills. All of the disclaimers said not to take them while pregnant for a reason.

After a few days of taking pills, I started to bleed accompanied by the most painful stomach cramps I had ever experienced. I was at my grandmother's house when it started and I told her it was just my period, which were usually brutal but nothing like this. I held it together until my mom picked me up to go home. Later on that evening, my mom came out of her room to find me lying on the floor in the fetal position, so she drove me to the emergency room.

We signed in and since I was in so much pain, they put me in wheelchair. We sat in the waiting room for hours. I told the front desk attendant that I needed to throw up, and they gave me a pot the size of a soup bowl to use. It wasn't big enough, so I ended up vomiting into the bowl and onto the floor. Someone came to clean up after me, and my mom demanded I be seen as soon as possible.

I had to throw up again, so that time she wheeled me to the door of the bathroom and I struggled to make my way to the stall by myself. After sitting down on the floor to throw up, I couldn't get back up. Repeatedly, I attempted to lift myself up but I just couldn't do it. My entire body was sweating, I was dizzy, and it felt like something was ripping through my stomach.

At a certain point, I stopped fighting to get off the floor by myself and pressed the emergency button in the stall. Shortly after, a nurse and my mom came in to get me. Once they picked me up and wheeled me back to be seen by a doctor, they asked me about my symptoms and if I was pregnant, to which I replied yes. They gave me pain medicine in an IV drip and drew blood.

About thirty minutes later, I went to the bathroom and felt a change in my body. I had a feeling it was over. The baby was gone. When I returned to the bed, the doctors confirmed it. They showed me a sheet of paper similar to the one I saw at my doctor's office when she told me I was pregnant. The emergency room doctor told me my hormone numbers were low, which meant I had a miscarriage.

All of the staff was remorseful. I never told them my plans to terminate my pregnancy, so they treated the situation delicately. I could even tell my mom was sad. She knew I hadn't planned on keeping the baby, but news of a miscarriage was still upsetting. I never told my mom or the doctors that I took birth control to try to terminate my pregnancy on my own. I didn't want them to judge or chastise me for going about it that way.

Weeks later, Josh called with some bullshit explanation about why he never returned any of my phone calls and that he was ready to help pay for the abortion. I simply told him not to worry about it and for him to never call me again. He desperately asked me what that meant as I hung up the phone.

When I returned to high school after winter break, I started wearing looser-fitting clothing to make myself less attractive to the opposite sex and kept to myself. When I tried to confide in a friend about what I had gone through, her response was so nonchalant that I never brought it up to anyone else. To be pregnant at such a young age was a big deal to me but apparently it wasn't as uncommon as I thought. There ended up being two girls pregnant at my school within the next few months.

Outside of hanging out with my friends during lunch break, I mainly kept my focus on school, work, and participating in drama club. I didn't drink, I didn't smoke, I didn't do drugs, and I was not having sex. I didn't even want a boy near me.

My math class was the only one I didn't have anyone I was friendly with in, so my conversations were limited to answering questions about our assignments. Class was lonely and boring but on the upside, it helped me stay focused on my classwork, which led to excellent grades.

There was a male Hispanic student who would always sit on the opposite side of the room. We didn't interact much aside from a rare 'hello', 'goodbye' or 'excuse me'. I never paid much attention to him until one day, out of the blue, he approached me as class was letting out to ask if I could go over some of the math lessons with him.

He seemed to be having a tough time so I agreed, maybe he was having difficulty following the teacher, since English wasn't his first language. While I helped him with math, he could teach me some Spanish.

He explained to me in broken English that his math textbook was downstairs in his locker and asked me to walk with him to get it. As we walked in the opposite direction of everyone leaving our class, I figured I would try to get to know him better by making small talk. As we talked, he led me down a stairwell in the back of the school towards a deserted locker bank near the less-frequented carpentry classes.

I continued to talk to him about how his other classes were going while he opened a locker and fumbled around inside. I looked around and began to wonder why none of the lockers in that area had locks on them. When I turned back towards him, he began grabbing my breast and trying to kiss me on the face and neck.

At first, I thought maybe our lines had been crossed due to the language barrier. I politely told him I wasn't interested but he continued to grab me to try and attempted to kiss me on the mouth. When I tried to push him away, he violently shoved his hand down the front of my pants. As he tried to get his hand inside of my underwear, I grabbed his arm and finally got him off me. I pushed him into the lockers and ran away towards the cafeteria, where I was scheduled to be after my math class.

Once I arrived, I found a teacher who was there overlooking the lunch room and explained to her what just happened. I could see the look of surprise on her face as she registered what I told her. At the time, I knew what he did was wrong and I felt violated. The teacher brought over an assistant principal who asked that I sit at an empty table and wait for her to locate the boy who had just accosted me.

Minutes later, they walked in with him and sat us at the exact same table, almost directly across from each other. As we sat there in silence, I kept my head down, trying not to make eye contact with him. Once the administrators were far enough away, he began to apologize profusely and tried to explain that it was just a misunderstanding. I stayed quiet, hoping none of the other students in the lunchroom knew what was going on.

Several uncomfortable minutes later, they walked us to the principal's waiting area, where we were put in separate rooms. I was instructed to write a report and was asked the same questions over and over about what happened by different staff. My grandmother was called to pick me up because I was in the office so long, I missed the bus home. The staff told her what happened, but I didn't want to discuss it with her.

Apparently, word got around at school that something happened to me, because a friend from the neighborhood next to my grandparents' walked over to check on me shortly after I had gotten home. I repeated the story to her once again, and she did her best to console me.

The next day in math class, the Hispanic boy wasn't there. Each day, I dreaded walking into class. I never knew if I was going to see him back in his seat on the other side of the room.

Once it was solidified that he wasn't coming back, I expected people to treat me differently. I didn't know who knew what information about our altercation, and I felt guilty for getting him kicked out of school. I started to second-guess myself. *Maybe I overreacted by reporting him. Maybe it was just a misunderstanding. Maybe I did or said something that made him think I wanted him to do that.* I didn't want to talk to anyone else about the incident, so I began to withdraw socially even more.

A few weeks later, my mom sat me down and told me I would have to testify about the incident at school. Before I did that, I would have to meet with someone who would prepare me for the trial. She took me to this historic area in downtown Annapolis where we walked into a building nearly completely made out of windows.

Once inside, we headed towards the legal office that prosecuted cases on behalf of the state involving minors. I was so nervous and didn't know what to expect. The entire situation was stressful for me.

A woman with shoulder-length brown hair came towards me smiling, wearing a suit and holding a file. She introduced herself as she walked us into her office. Once inside, she explained that I would be a witness in the trial regarding the boy from my class who touched me inappropriately. She asked me to tell her everything that happened, even though she already had a copy of my written statement. I was uncomfortable repeating the story again but was relieved that my mom was sitting outside the room. I couldn't bear to tell what happened in front of her.

After detailing my account of what happened, the attorney went over some questions I would be asked while in the courtroom. She told me to try not to say "I don't know" or "Ummm" when responding to questions. If I wasn't sure, it was best to simply ask for more time, and then try to answer carefully and honestly. She also told me that the boy from my class and I wouldn't be in the courtroom at the same time, so I wouldn't have to worry about seeing him. On the way out, she informed us of the date I would need to come back to that same building for the trial.

When we returned on the date provided, that was my first time in a courtroom. My grandfather, grandmother, and mom were all there with me. We sat outside of the room my case was being handled in for a very long time. The state's attorney would come out every so often to keep us updated on what was happening inside the courtroom.

Before it was time for me to testify, the Hispanic boy from my math class and his family walked out of the courtroom and sat down on a bench on the far side of the lobby. I didn't tell my family he was the one responsible for us being there. I tried to catch his eye to see if he was remorseful or angry, or if he even understood the severity of the situation, because I didn't. He never looked in my direction.

Finally, the time came for me to go in and tell my story. My family sat in the courtroom as I gave my recollection of what happened in the abandoned locker bank of my school. After I answered all of the questions, my family and I went back into the waiting area until the judge asked for any last comments. The state's attorney asked if we wanted to enter to make any last statements, and we did.

When the judge asked if anyone from my family would like to say anything, my grandfather stood up. He spoke to my character, how close our family was, and how this incident had affected our family. As he spoke, he began to cry.

Aside from when my grandfather's mother and sister passed away, I never saw him cry. My family was a loving one, but not necessarily an emotional one. Even though I didn't express how being violated affected me, my grandfather was in pain for me. It hurt my heart to see how what happened to me could cause him so much pain.

In the end, the judge praised me on the way I answered questions and carried myself in such a serious situation. They found the young man guilty, but I didn't understand what the charges were or what punishment he would face afterwards. No one at school ever mentioned him or seemed to notice that he never returned to class.

The pain I saw on my family's faces that day was too much for me to bear. I felt like I had brought that pain on them, even though I didn't do anything wrong. If anything like that ever happened again, I vowed to shield them from knowing, because I couldn't see those looks on their faces again.

CHAPTER 4

2003

Since my last year of high school consisted of nothing but electives and I only needed to take three classes to graduate, I was finished by ten in the morning. After my classes were done, I had the choice to work or take college courses, but I decided to do both. Each day, I would take classes at my county's community college then work part-time at whichever job was available at the mall.

While at school, I was actively involved in compiling photos and articles for my senior yearbook, and I was also still active in the drama club. The relationships I had developed over my four years in high school felt superficial. Most of the kids in my high school had been friends since before I started public school. The people I thought were my friends would change whenever the wind blew a new guy in their direction. I had never fully developed a sense of loyalty with anyone.

I thought going to prom and participating in senior activities would redeem my overall experience, so I opted out of graduating a year early so I could spend more time bonding with my graduating class and try to build new friendships. Instead, my senior year was a huge disappointment.

For prom, my grandmother wouldn't let me get the

dress I really wanted. It was almost a replica of the dress Halle Berry wore when she won her Oscar. Instead, I ended up showing up to prom wearing the same dress as another classmate

My date, who didn't even attend my school, spent all of his money on a new tux, which meant he didn't help me pay for the tickets or pictures. I resented my date so much for spending all his money on a tux for a prom that wasn't his that I barely spoke to him the entire night. I made him drop me off at home immediately after the dance to sulk in disappointment alone.

I did attend graduation with standings at the top of my class, but I was in such a rush to make it there on time that I didn't eat. While waiting in the holding area, lined up to head to our seats in alphabetical order, I started to feel light-headed. I figured it was just nerves and hopefully by the time I made it to my seat, I would feel better.

Instead, the dizziness got worse. The room was starting to spin, and I thought I was going to pass out. They repeatedly instructed us to stay in our seats, but I thought it was better for me to pass out in the back rather than in front of my entire class and their families.

As I walked back towards the holding area, a teacher came to see what was wrong. At the same time, my mother came down from the bleachers. She saw me walk out and knew something was wrong. I described to them how I was feeling, and they both recommended I eat or drink something with sugar.

There my mom was, to the rescue. She had a granola bar in her purse, and the teacher retrieved a Sprite from the vending machine. As the color came back to my face, I wished then more than ever that I had just graduated a year early and left my delusions of missing out on an amazing senior year behind.

Around the time I was finishing up high school, I began working at a new restaurant near the mall down the road from my grandparents' house. There was a girl who lived in the court behind their house young named Nayla who went through training with me. She was a couple of years older than me so we were never close in high school, but we ended up bonding at work and became inseparable.

It never bothered me to be around other attractive people, except for Nayla. When people asked her, "What are you?" she would always respond that she was Black but left out the fact that her mother was mixed with Black and White and her father was Trinidadian and Hawaiian. The mixture contributed to her exotic look of curly hair and light skin. Add in her beautiful face, naturally flat stomach, curvy shape, and perky boobs and was always the center of attention in any room.

Over time, I had gotten comfortable enough to describe myself as an attractive woman. I didn't have a problem with the way I looked but if I there was anyone I would be self-conscious around, it was her. When I went out with her, it was like I instantly faded into the background. I know that all women can't appeal to every man's taste, but she never had a problem finding a guy interested in her.

We each seemed to attract very different types of men. I got mainly older, overweight, short, unattractive, or disrespectful men. She enticed physically attractive, charismatic, polished, and successful men. Although I would have been described as having a 'Coke bottle' shape with hips, a decent-size butt and boobs, I always felt like I wasn't skinny enough, my skin wasn't light enough, or my hair wasn't good enough when I was around her.

When she would talk about how she needed to lose twenty

pounds or how much she hated her hair, it would really bother me, because I was heavier than her and tried so many products to get my hair like hers. I would give anything to have her shape. It would make me think, if she needs to lose twenty pounds then was I obese? She had men throwing themselves at her left and right, people staring as she walked by, with men and women alike complimenting her looks, but it wasn't enough for her.

She and I would frequently go out to various clubs in DC, then during our time off, we would travel to different cities together to party. No matter where we were, I noticed that men were looking straight through me to stare at her. Guys would keep their eyes glued to her, even if they were addressing me. People would walk by and say to her "you're so beautiful" as I stood next to her, feeling like an imaginary friend.

Going out so frequently in our late teens and early twenties allowed us to build a rapport with most of the security guards around DC, which ensured expedited entry and special treatment. Before I was of legal drinking age, I would frequently bypass the '21 and over' rule by using Nayla's ID. We lived it up almost every weekend, mingling at each bar or flirting amongst the bottle service tables when celebrity hosts were in town.

In the Washington DC area, and usually the beautiful women outnumbered the handsome men. So while at the club, I would try to catch the eye of one of the few good-looking guys who hadn't already found a girl for the night. After exchanging a few coy glances, he would begin to walk in my direction. I would quickly reapply my lip gloss and make sure my outfit was accentuating all the right places as the guy would continue to walk past me and approach Nayla.

The constant silent treatment and brush-overs made me

consider throwing my ideal list of qualities for the man I wanted to date out the window. It seemed like no matter how much effort I put into making myself up, it was never good enough. Maybe I was always going to have to settle for the 'less attractive friend' or whatever was left after the girls who looked like Nayla had gotten the cream of the crop.

I didn't need to date a model but I did want to find the guy I was dating attractive. I was drawn to a certain type of guy. Scanning a room, I would immediately be drawn to maybe only one or two men—my taste was particular.

Maybe I would never get the whole package: looks, brains, personality, maturity, respect, honesty, and consistency. When I did make the acquaintance of a man, he would just be looking for sex. With the way men were treating women those days, it appeared I was going to be single for a very long time.

Nayla, on the other hand, met so many eligible bachelors that she had more guys pursuing her than she knew what to do with. Athletes, singers, rappers, business owners—you name it and they wanted to be with her. There would always be a new guy buying her gifts or a plane ticket to come see them. Certain guys were only around for a few weeks, but others would stick around for years.

One of her main love interests was Zeke Collins—everyone called him Z for short. He was tall, dark and handsome but with a mediocre sense of style and a cocky attitude. He was a football player who grew up in Maryland but moved away to play professionally. He frequently made it a point to come back to town and take all of his boys to the club.

His looks would draw women in, but his behavior was a major turn-off. One night, he invited Nayla to a club in DC and she brought me along. The entire time we were there, the two of them played this game where they acted like the other person wasn't important. She would flirt with guys in clear view of him, and he would have some girl hanging around his table so Nayla could see.

Upon leaving, the two of them started arguing over the way the other behaved the entire night. Bickering outside of the club had become a reoccurring habit. Even though they weren't in a committed relationship, they clearly cared about each other and would get upset if the other person didn't show them enough attention.

The entire group migrated from the front of the club towards where she and I were parked. His friends stood by and did nothing to calm him down or move him towards the limo they rented every time they went out. No matter how irrational or ignorant Z would get, his friends never corrected him or tried to stop him.

It was like he held all of the power, and if they spoke up he would kick them out of the group. Sometimes, I thought he was a cult leader and they were his followers. I guess because he made the most money and bought the tables at clubs, they did whatever he said.

As the two of them continued to make a scene in the middle of the street, a cab driver saw what was happening and attempted to save us from what he perceived as a hostile situation. He yelled out his passenger side window that he would offer us ladies a free cab ride to our car. Z took great offense to the idea of the guy thinking he was a threat, and proceeded to berate him. Yelling at him, "My watch could buy three of your cabs. Get the fuck out of here!" The cab driver reluctantly drove off; no matter how much he wanted to save us, he was outnumbered.

We all stood by nervously, not knowing when this episode

was going to end. Once Z began to speak in a demeaning manner towards Nayla, I decided things were going too far. I got between them, trying to move her towards our car as I told them to table the conversation until they were both sober. He responded by telling me to mind my own business and get out of the way.

As if this was a command, his friends came over to move me away from them. I couldn't believe what was unfolding before my eyes. They would keep me from trying to interject and end the argument, but wouldn't do a single thing to stop him from aggressively berating a female in the middle of the street.

No matter how volatile or unhealthy their relationship got, they never stayed away from each other for long. She would say she was done with him and then a few days later, she would ask me if I wanted to meet up with him and his friends because he had booked another bottle service table.

During the football season, she would travel to NY to stay with him and attend his home games. Even though they never actually made it official, their courtship was enough drama for a reality TV show. Maybe if they had met a decade later, when they both were more mature, they could've been happy together.

During one of her hiatuses from Z, Nayla found another man to occupy her time. She met an up-and-coming football player named Jett Richards during one of our nights out. When they met, he had just been signed and was eager to flash his newly earned riches. Having a beautiful girl on his arm was just what he needed to complete his image.

Their relationship was much less dramatic than the one she had with Z, which at times left Nayla bored. She had to travel frequently to see him in Minnesota. She even became close with his friends and family by spending so much time there. I thought Jett could be the one for her. She seemed to be building a nice little life with him. He incorporated her into his life, there were no below-the-belt blow-outs, and he seemed ready to settle down.

Since I was so unlucky with men, Nayla was always trying to set me up with a friend of the guy she was currently dating or a guy she wasn't interested in. I would always give them a chance, but inevitably our communication would dwindle to nothing. Jett had a new teammate who was on the practice squad named Jason. Nayla couldn't wait to introduce us. Even though they'd just met, Jett spoke very highly of him.

Jason and I started out talking on the phone and sent each other photos via text. I would always inquire about when we would see each other but he would put it off, blaming his football schedule, family visits, or his living situation. Since he had yet to officially be signed to the team, he was staying in a hotel with a roommate. Once he was given the green light to move into a condo, we both agreed on a weekend when I would come visit him.

The first night of my visit was spent in a hotel room because his condo was bare; his furniture was being delivered the next day. He dropped me off on the way to practice the next morning and I walked into a bare-bones apartment. There was no bed, no living room furniture, no kitchenware, or food. The only things there were a blanket on the floor, a small TV, and a DVD player. He gave me the responsibility of being the one to sign for the furniture when it was delivered and gave me some money for takeout.

The night before, his roommate and his girlfriend had spent the night sleeping on the floor, watching TV. Since I couldn't go back to sleep, I decided to peruse their movie selection. When I opened the DVD player, there was already a disk in there. It was unmarked, and since black people frequently had the latest and greatest bootleg movies, I pressed play to see what they had been watching.

It took a little while for the movie to start then a black man with a beer gut and tattoos, wearing a Zorro mask, cape, and black boxer briefs, came on the screen. I thought to myself, this doesn't look like any box office movie I've ever seen a preview for. The film was of poor quality, set in someone's living room like a home movie. As the movie continued, a thick black woman, wearing a Mardi Gras mask, appeared on the screen and sat on the couch. As the next few seconds went by, I realized it was a low-budget porno.

It didn't seem right for me to continue watching as I sat there by myself at eight o'clock in the morning, so I immediately took it out. I tried my luck with the next unmarked disk sitting near the DVD player. This one started with a house party, so I continued watching. Moments later, everyone in the movie began getting undressed, running from room to room seeking someone to have sex with. I had come to the determination that Jason's roommate was a freak.

My next selection was required to actually have a title printed on the disc by a legitimate production company before I entered it into the DVD player. Shortly after I finished watching my second movie, the furniture arrived. I was more excited than I should have been as I eagerly awaited the delivery guys to set up all of the furniture. They assembled his bed and staged the living room furniture as I instructed.

The rest of my trip was uneventful, but he and I seemed to bond over decorating his first apartment. After I came back home, our communication dwindled. In my mind, I thought we grew closer during my trip to Minnesota and thought maybe if I went back to visit him, it would rekindle that bond. Being overeager and naïve at that age, I planned on booking a flight to surprise him.

By the time I went to book my trip, Nayla and I had stopped speaking because of some petty falling-out. We would frequently get mad over something insignificant and ignore each other for a few days. In the end, neither of us could remember why we weren't talking and would break the ice during one of our shifts at work.

One afternoon, she overheard me talking about the trip I was planning to visit Jason. Once I was alone, she came over to me and said, "I heard about your plans to go back to Minnesota and when I told Jett about it, he said you should reconsider. Jett didn't know it when we set you up, but Jason has a girlfriend and she's going to be in town this month."

I tried not to seem surprised and hurt, but I should've known something wasn't right by the way Jason was behaving. I still needed to verify what she told me, so I simply thanked her for the warning then walked away. She was either trying to be a good friend despite our falling-out, or she was being spiteful to sabotage my trip.

I took a break and called Jason to ask him outright. He paused for a moment then confirmed he had a long-distance girlfriend from college. He claimed they had been having problems, but I told him that wasn't an excuse to keep that information from me. Once again, I had been played.

Why would he tell me had a girlfriend? I was just a meaningless girl from Maryland who made it easy for him to use her. You can't really see all of the signs from hundreds of miles away, but that explained why our communication was so sporadic and why it was never a good time for me to come see him.

The nearly disastrous trip Nayla prevented broke the ice

for us to resume our friendship. Immediately, she was there to support me and bash him. It wasn't long before we started hanging out again, as if we were never upset with each other. She suggested that we head out to a particular club in DC we frequented called Play to take my mind off how miserable my dating record was.

Play was a three-level club which I considered to be two levels, because the bottom floor was dedicated to reggae music but it no lights except at the bar. I hated walking down there because it gave men the freedom to roam the pitch-black room and inappropriately grab women then disappear into the darkness. The middle level was where the main entrance and dance floor was, and the top level had a balcony which led to an exclusive VIP area.

We would go there so frequently that all of the bouncers knew us by name and would let us go into the VIP area whether we had the required wristbands or not. I was under twenty-one so at the door they would put a huge, black "X" on my hand to indicate I was under drinking age. As soon I got in, I would walk straight to the bathroom, wash off the marker, and head to the bar.

The bartenders weren't as fond of us. They were all females, and their attention went to the men who were usually footing the tabs at the bar. We would stand at the bar ready to order ourselves a drink but it never failed that a guy would offer to buy us one. We got in for free, drank for free, and partied in VIP for free. Why wouldn't we keep coming back?

Almost weekly, Nayla and I would meet local artists, club promoters, athletes, or celebrities in the VIP area. There was always someone in town for a sports game or to perform at a local venue. One night, I met not one but two college athletes who seemed to get the attention and perks of professionals.

The first one was a cocky, muscular guy of average height who played football for Maryland State University named Kevin. Upon speaking with him, I told him he looked familiar and he said it may have been because I had seen him out. I knew that wasn't true because if I *had* seen him out, we would've met already. Later on, I found out he looked so familiar because he was the younger brother —and spitting image—of one the most impressive defensive players for the local NFL team.

The other guy, Curt, was also a Maryland State athlete, but he was a basketball player. He was extremely tall and lanky with the face of a mischievous little boy and a smile that would—and frequently did—charm the pants off any woman he encountered. I could tell that both of them were full of themselves and were used to getting whatever they wanted.

They were both adored by women of all ages and given special privileges locally and on campus. Since I didn't go to their school, I didn't know who they were before I met them or how successful they were at playing their respective sports—nor did I care. I maintained contact with both of them for a while until I could figure out which one was going to give me less trouble.

CHAPTER 5

2005

I graduated from community college two years after high school, but I didn't have a clear idea of what I wanted to do afterwards. One of the girls from my job threw out the idea of us both going to school together at Maryland State. I hadn't been looking forward to more tests, deadlines, and other demands of continuing education, but going through it with someone else eased my hesitation.

Waiting to get a response from the school, we discussed how much fun we were going to have. We made plans to find an apartment together, talked about splitting the cost of groceries and how much we would party at the infamous campus bars. She actually got me excited about going back to school.

A few weeks later, I received a letter in the mail stating that I was accepted. When I went to tell her the good news, she informed me that she decided not to attend full-time and would only be taking one or two classes a semester. I didn't even want to apply in the first place. After weeks of being convinced to take on something I wasn't sure I even wanted, I found myself facing such a major commitment alone.

When the fall semester started, there I was at a new school with zero friends to hang out with on campus. If anyone I knew from high school was there, they had already been there for two years while I was in community college, so I was sure they would have a new circle of friends. I didn't attend orientation because I wasn't coming in as a freshman, so I didn't have the opportunity to meet other incoming students there. My first few days on campus were very lonely.

The only people I was familiar with on campus were Kevin and Curt. Once I reconnected with them and told them I would be attending their school, they welcomed me to hang out with them and their teammates, I quickly felt like 'one of the guys'. Even though we would all sit together during lunch breaks, they were generally busy with class, tutors, and practice, which meant I still needed to find other friends.

I happened to receive a flier in the mail that was sent to new students about a 'Fall Rush' sorority event. It was a series of days where the sororities that had houses on campus hosted an open house for new students to walk door to door and interview to become a member. The historically black sororities at my school were really difficult to get into unless you knew someone in them, which I didn't, so this seemed like my best option to make new friends.

All of the sorority houses I went to were full of nothing but blonde girls in frilly dresses with pearls hanging around their necks and BMWs in the driveways. I felt like the black Goldilocks. *This house is too preppy. This house is too boring. This house is too stuck-up.* By the time I reached the last house I was willing to visit that day, I thought I had made a mistake. There was no way I would find a place where I fit in.

Luckily for me, the last one felt just right. I ended up feeling the most comfortable at the Sigma Phi Alpha sorority. There was one black girl and one mixed girl who already were members, which were one and a half more black girls than I encountered at any other house I visited.

Finding a house I liked was only half of the battle. After the initial rush, each sorority narrowed down the list of girls they wanted to invite back and called them in for a more personalized visit. After the second visit, only a handful of girls were going to be accepted into that sorority.

One afternoon after class, my phone rang and when I answered, I was greeted by a very excited girl on the other end that I didn't recognize. She gladly informed me that they were extending a membership to Alpha Delta Pi. That was the only house I would've accepted, so I immediately told her how excited I was to join. Once I began participating in activities with the sorority and got the hang of my classes, my college experience started looking up.

Over the next few weeks of getting to know the girls, I noticed the house had a lot of cliques. From the little I had known about sororities, I thought it was supposed to feel like a group of sisters who were building lifelong connections. Sometimes when I went to the house, I felt like a visitor in a stranger's home. They allowed me to sit on their couch, offered me food and snacks, but it wasn't as if we actually knew each other.

There were only a handful of girls who took the time out to get to know me. Kira was a fan of our school's sports teams, so we bonded over that. We had similar personalities and interests, so we ended up becoming really close. We even won an award at one of the sorority events for being 'Most Attached at the Hip'.

Every Tuesday and Thursday, Kira and I would have lunch together with some of the guys from the football team in the school cafeteria. Outside of sports, she and I would bond over boy troubles or common feelings about not fitting in at the sorority. Every girl in the sorority salivated over any story they could get out of us about the athletes at school. They were our campus' superstars, no matter what sport.

Most of the other girls weren't huge sports fans but were fans of pregaming, so we would religiously attend games together. I was the one who would sit outside the stadium, no matter the weather, for two hours before every home basketball game so I could save us the front row seats that were the hardest to get. There was a particular event staff member who became so fond us of he would even save seats for us during popular rivalry games.

Even though we all watched the football and basketball games from the bleachers, I felt like part of a more exclusive club since I got to eat lunch with the players twice a week. Girls would walk by and try to get the football players' attention, but Kira and I didn't have to try; we were a welcome addition to their table. Everyone would crack jokes and tell stories in between stuffing their faces before the next class. As a natural progression, Kira and I eventually began hanging out with the players outside of the cafeteria, as well.

There were a few times when we would head out to the college bars as a part of their entourage or hang out in a player's dorm room and drink before going out. It became more comfortable spending time with the guys than at the sorority house. Females too often gossiped, backstabbed, or ruined friendships over jealousy and pettiness.

With the guys, I didn't feel they had any ulterior motives and never felt pressured to do things I didn't want to do. I just felt like one of them. Since I had relationship romantic in nature with Kevin, there didn't seem to be any problems keeping things platonic with other guys from the team.

My first few months on campus, I split my time with Kevin from the football team and Curt from the basketball team. Curt took up more of my time when I first got to campus because I was more fond of his personality. He was like the kid on the playground everyone wanted to play with because of his jovial attitude. After a night out at the campus bars, I would end up back at his dorm and wouldn't head home until the next morning. Sometimes, he would invite me out with him and his teammates, but we never went out on dates or hung out outside of campus.

He was very particular about being intimate. He said he didn't just kiss anyone, so it took a while for us to lock lips, which was a turn-off for me because I loved kissing, I could kiss someone all night without doing anything else and be satisfied. Since he hooked up with so many women, I guess that was his way of keeping something sacred.

Without much foreplay, sex with Curt wasn't particularly enjoyable. He was too quick to climax and he wasn't well endowed. When I realized our mediocre casual sex wasn't going to turn into anything more, I had to deal with only being a hookup or leave him alone. After hearing rumors about him around campus of having a kid on the way and that he was failing out of his classes, it only made sense to leave him alone.

I stopped by his dorm one day because he asked me for notes from a criminal justice class we shared. While he was in the bathroom, I noticed a picture of a baby taped to his wall. Had I not noticed it before because I had never been to his room in the daylight, or did he just put it up there? Once he returned, I asked who the little boy was and he told me it was his son.

At first, I thought he was joking, but his facial expression told me he wasn't. I looked at him and saw just a kid, a kid in a man's body. As I walked away, I was grateful it wasn't me who had to deal with raising his kid while waiting for him to grow up.

Even though we were no longer hooking up, I would still run into him since Nayla was hooking up with his suitemate, Nick. One night out, we ended up back in their dorm room. Nick had invited Nayla over after running into her at Play. She dragged me along because she didn't want to go by herself. I had been very diligent about not contacting Curt and decided that even if I did see him, I would stay strong and keep my legs closed.

While Nayla was in Nick's room, I sat in the common area by myself. There was no TV so I laid on the couch, waiting for her to come back out. A few minutes into my solitude, a small Asian girl holding books and carrying a backpack darted straight out of Curt's room and exited out the front door. She got out of there so fast, if had blinked I would've missed her.

Not long after, Curt walked out into the common area, surveyed the room, and spotted me sitting there. I'm sure he was shocked to see me there by myself. We exchanged hellos, and I explained that I was simply waiting for Nayla to come out of his friend's room. After a long pause, he asked, "Why don't you wait in my room?"

I had made some questionable decisions in the past, but I respected myself enough not to go into his bedroom directly after another girl just left. I mentioned that I saw the young lady who had just scurried out of his room. He responded with they were just 'studying'. As he stood there with his shirt off, he would have fed me any lie to get me in his room.

No one runs out of a room like that after simply going over school work. I continued to decline his repeated invitations into his room for several minutes until he had the audacity to say, "If you don't come in here, I'll call another girl to come over." The only thing I could do was laugh because no matter how ridiculous this statement was, I knew he was being serious.

He retrieved his phone out of his room and started dialing in front of me. I sat back, closed my eyes, and tried to tune him out. Once a girl answered, he took the phone call into his room. A few minutes later, he came out wearing nothing but boxer briefs with his standard goofy grin plastered on his face. He warned me that it was my last chance to change my mind. If I agreed, he would call the girl who was on her way and tell her not to come.

I knew I had to be firm with him; otherwise, he would keep trying to chip away at my sanity. I stood my ground and tried to drown out everything else he was saying. About fifteen minutes later, there was a knock at the door. He came out of his room and paused to look at me before letting the girl in. I'm sure he thought drama was going to ensue, but I wasn't going to participate in the game he was playing. Long before that night, I figured out the kind of guy Curt was and acknowledged that he wasn't good for me.

Not long after that night, Curt's teammate told me he was spiraling out of control from drinking too much and as a result he was failing most of his classes. Instead of trying to improve his current situation, he was going to try his hand at playing professionally. All of the comments I would overhear from students were about how embarrassing it was that he had failed out of school with everything he had going for him. There were high hopes that he was going to make it to the NBA after he completed college and improved his stats. He never ended up reaching his full potential.

My relationship with Kevin had slightly more substance, even though when I first met him I couldn't stand him. The night we met, Nayla had also exchanged information with one of his friends. If she wanted to hang out with his friend, I ended up tagging along, being forced to spend time with him. He was arrogant and walked around like the world owed him something.

Even though his older brother was an NFL player, he didn't want to use that as a crutch. He wanted to be taken seriously because of his own talent, which may have been the reason he tried to overcompensate not only on the field but off. It was all about showing off what he had and what he could do. Which was why he rubbed me the wrong way.

After I started spending less time with Curt, I reconnected with Kevin and we decided to start over. Through spending more time together, we began to enjoy being around each other. I would go to class, complete my sorority commitments, and head straight to his apartment. We would spend several evenings together a week hanging out and hooking up.

Everything would seem great for a while and then I would go days without hearing from him. I knew his priorities were class, practices, games, and his daughter, who he tried to spend as much time with as possible. Then there was me, dead last on his list of priorities. I accepted whatever time he would give me in the hopes that my dedication to him would pay off in the end.

Month after month, it became more unpredictable when I would hear from him or see him, even though we spent five days a week on the same campus. I recognized that he was a football player with unlimited options of women, so I didn't want to nag him into the arms of some other girl. My focus turned to my classes, work, and my sorority activities as I waited around, hoping he would message me to hang out.

Most of his teammates knew we were together in some capacity, so they usually greeted me with a warm welcome and invited me along whenever I saw them out. Of course, there was always the handful of guys who didn't know or just didn't care. They would try to see how far they could get with me, but I wrote them off as harmless flirts.

The guys from the football team had such explosive personalities that I couldn't help but have a good time with them. They always supplied liquor and laughs, which kept nights interesting. Not to mention they were royalty at all of the local campus bars and clubs. Athletes were the elite of our campus, and to be friends with them offered unique experiences.

One chilly April night during my second semester, Kira and I met a few players in their dorm room for a bit of drinking prior to heading out to the campus bars. We were drinking mixed drinks, taking shots of E&J, laughing uncontrollably and dancing in our seats to the radio. Even though the night was just getting started, it didn't seem like it could get any better.

We spent longer than expected drinking in the dorms but finally decided to take a walk to the main road where all of the bars were located. The guys chose to head to the most popular bar, Crossroads, but security wouldn't let all of us in because they were over capacity. Instead of leaving anyone behind, we headed to the bar next door, which was dead. The group then headed over to the pizza place across the street where most people ended up to soak up the alcohol.

Kira and I weren't eating, so we left with two of the football players to try and catch last call somewhere. Once we got outside, the guys started walking up the hill towards the dorms. It was getting late, and the guys didn't think it was worth it to try another club. On the way back Kira stopped to talk to someone she knew from one of her classes with some of the football players. I continued walking ahead alone with a guy who was a regular at our lunch gatherings named Jake. I was so drunk I started to complain nonstop to him about being tired and cold. We were walking slowly to give the others time to catch up, but they were taking forever. I started yelling at Kira to come on, but she didn't budge.

Jake and I had never spent any time alone together before and, to be quite honest, even though I knew he had a girlfriend, I always wondered if he was gay. He offered to take me back to his room so I could get warm and wait for everyone to join us. I didn't really have any other options since I didn't live on campus and was too drunk to drive home, so I followed him. He put his arm around me in an attempt to keep me warm as we made our way to his building.

Once inside his room, I asked where I could lie down while we waited for our group to arrive. He told me I could lie on his bed, but first I had to help him clean it off. I really wasn't in the mood to clean someone else's mess, but I was willing to help him if it meant I could lay down. He handed me some shirts that were on his bed and asked me to fold them.

As he turned on the TV, I got a text from Kira asking where I was and I told her I was in Jake's dorm room. She replied that she was still outside waiting on some of the other players. I texted her to come get me because Jake was getting on my nerves. I wasn't in the mood to be around him anymore.

As soon as I finished sending that text, he told me to put my phone away so we could lie down. I didn't understand why it mattered, but I decided not to argue with him about it. I tucked my phone away in my purse and put it on vibrate so he wouldn't know when it went off. I went to lie on the side of the bed, but he immediately told me to get up. He informed me that he had really bad allergies, so I wasn't allowed to be on his bed with my clothes on since they were 'covered with pollen'.

At that point, I came to the conclusion that he regretted his decision to invite me to his room and was doing everything he could to get me to leave without actually kicking me out. I bluntly asked him why he was acting so strangely. If there was a problem with me being there, I would gladly wait outside. He said everything was fine but I had made up my mind to just wait in the common area until Kira came.

He assured me he wasn't trying to get me to leave and that he would give me a set of his clothes to wear instead. I wanted to accommodate his bizarre requests because the alcohol had caught up to me and it was getting harder to stay standing. Before I was going to take off the clothes I had on, he needed to give me something to change into first.

He started giving me a hard time about handing over the clothes in an attempt to be funny, until he saw I wasn't in a joking mood. Finally, he gave me a white t-shirt and some athletic shorts to wear. I did a quick high school locker room-style change without exposing my underwear while he changed on the other side of the room. I thought I was in the clear, but he stopped me once again to tell me I also had to take off my bra because it had been exposed to pollen.

His requests were becoming more and more ridiculous. As tired and intoxicated as I was, I didn't want to go back and forth about my clothes; I just wanted to rest. I began to feel more and more uncomfortable about being there. I had no desire to take off any of my clothes, especially not my underwear. I wanted to respect his space, but there was a line between a reasonable request and an outlandish demand.

"I swear, if you do this one last thing, we can lie down." To silence my urge to immediately put my clothes back on and leave. I assured myself that he was not a threat to me and that he was just an odd person. After having a standoff in the middle of his room for several minutes, I finally removed my bra from under the white t-shirt. The green light to lie down was finally given.

I stayed on the opposite side of the bed, directly against the wall, and discreetly made a move for my phone. My purse was next to me with my phone hidden behind it. I texted Kira that Jake was really strange and I really wanted to leave. I told her the building and dorm number and emphasized that she hurry.

As soon as I put my phone back into my purse, Jake turned the TV off and pulled me closer to him. I told him I just wanted to lie down in peace and that there was no desire on my end to be intimate with him. So I scooted back over to my original position against the wall. He assured me he just wanted to cuddle and wasn't going to try anything.

I laid as still as possible and closed my eyes in an attempt to get him to leave me alone, but he continued to pull on me. In my debilitated state of mind, I tried to think of every excuse I could give him to leave me alone. I checked my phone again while it was still tucked behind my bag and saw Kira had texted me, letting me know she was on the way.

Finally, help was coming. As I got ready to tell him I was going to get dressed and wait for Kira in the common area, Jake rolled on top of me. I didn't know what was happening, I was so caught off-guard. We had never kissed, never flirted, and never even had a conversation before that night.

His actions came out of nowhere. As far as I knew, he had a girlfriend and he seemed like he was faithful to her. I had never even seen him with another girl, and he definitely had showed no prior interest in me. I tried to make it clear to all the guys that I wasn't interested in fooling around with anyone from the football team other than Kevin.

After all of the time I spent rebuilding a bond with Kevin, I wasn't going to throw that away on some guy I wasn't even attracted to. Aside from the man of my dreams being on the football team, I wasn't going to hook up with anyone else. There was no way I was going to be the girl they thought they could pass around.

As soon as he ignored my initial request to get off me, I attempted to push him off. I told him Kira was on the way and I was ready to leave. He didn't budge; he just kept grabbing my face in an attempt to kiss me. I continued to move my face away from his mouth while squirming my entire body to try and get from under him.

Seeing how this guy was in the gym almost every day and his job on the field was to repeatedly tackle grown men twice my size to the ground, I was unsuccessful. Trying to physically overpower him wasn't working, so my next line of defense was to try and talk some sense into him. I kept pleading with him to get off me while still trying my best to push him away. Maybe he was drunk and thought I was playing hard to get, so I kept trying everything I could to make it clear I didn't want him.

I tried reasoning with him, but he had a rebuttal for everything. I told him I had a relationship with his teammate and I wasn't going to do anything to jeopardize that. He responded with, "What does he have to do with me? It doesn't matter since you aren't his girlfriend." Then I brought up *his* girlfriend and that she would be upset if he cheated on her. He replied, "My girlfriend and I have an understanding; since we're in different cities, we can sleep with other people."

My second line of defense wasn't working any better than

my first. It would have been different if I were kissing him and reciprocating the affection, but I never did anything to indicate I was romantically interested in him. Not only was I trying to push him off me, I was giving him every reason I could think of to stop what he was doing. There was no confusion about whether or not I wanted him to get off me, but he wouldn't.

The weight of his body was pressing on my torso and it began to feel like I was having an anxiety attack. The room was pitch black, there was a man I didn't want pinning me down, touching me in ways I didn't want to be touched, I was drunk, and I felt helpless. To make matters worse, he started to try and take the shirt I was wearing off.

At that point, I realized I needed to put my defenses into overdrive. This started off as what I thought was an innocent miscommunication then switched into a scary situation I wasn't sure how to get out of. I was fearful of what was going to happen if I couldn't stop him.

In a loud and firm tone I repeated that I didn't want to sleep with him, I didn't want him touching me and for him to get off of me. I kept repeating over and over that I just came there to sleep but now I wanted to leave. I reminded him that I told Kira where I was and she would be there any minute so I needed to get dressed. That should have been enough for him to stop, but he ignored my pleading, continuing to kiss and lick on my neck and face.

Everywhere he touched me made my skin crawl. Whenever he tried to kiss my face, I would move away and try to slide from underneath him. Getting fed up with my resistance, he immobilized my face by holding it still with both of his hands. I could feel my phone vibrating on the bed and desperately tried to free at least one hand to retrieve it, but my arm couldn't reach out far enough.

The weight of his body felt like it was pushing the air out of me. He had my legs pinned between the inside of his thighs. I was able to wedge my arms between our chests to keep him from lying directly on top of me. No matter how I tried to push him off me, I couldn't make him budge. He wouldn't stop grabbing at my shirt, trying to get under the clothes I was wearing, holding on to my face, licking me, kissing me.

I was being tormented and I could feel the walls closing in on me. The room was so dark that I couldn't even see his face. All I could see when I looked around the room was the light coming through the blinds over my head from the street lamps. He took away physical control of my body and wouldn't stop no matter how much I tried. For a moment, silence fell over the room. As I tried to keep up my defenses, tears began to run down my face.

I didn't know what would happen if I hit him in the face or screamed for help. The less I did to anger him, the better off I thought I would be. It seemed like I had been trapped under him for hours; I was physically and emotionally drained. I kept hoping Kira would come through the door to save me but it was just me. Alone. Fighting to free myself.

I demanded to know why he was doing this to me. He didn't respond. I had given him every reason I could think of to stop. I had been physically trying to resist him since he first put his hands on me. The longer this went on, I was positive that he was going to rape me.

The shirt and shorts he gave me were so loose-fitting that it was easy for him to slide his hands underneath, onto my skin. He kept putting his hand in through the bottom of the shorts. All of a sudden, I felt something trying to penetrate my vagina and my panic went through the roof.

I didn't know if it was his hand or his penis, but I had to kick my self-preservation into overdrive. With all the force I had, I moved my pelvis away from him and started screaming. The thought of him trying to have unprotected sex with me sent me over the edge. The possibility of him giving me a disease or having any of his fluids getting near me made me want to vomit.

Then it happened—someone knocked at the main door of his dorm. I told him Kira was at the door and to get off me immediately. He simply rolled over to the other side of the bed like it was nothing. I jumped up, quickly gathered my clothes and rushed to change out of his clothing. By the time I had finished putting my sweater on over my shirt, Kira knocked on his door and entered his room.

I quietly made my way behind her into the common area as she made small talk with Jake. With no sign of aggression in his voice, he spoke as if he'd had the most relaxing, uneventful evening. She and I finally left his room and walked into the hallway. After pushing the down button to retrieve the elevator, I did my best to explain to her what I had just experienced but couldn't find the right words.

I asked her if she had ever been in a situation where a guy had done things to her she didn't want. She nonchalantly said, "Sure." She made it seem like that kind of thing happened all of time. I didn't know how to process what I was feeling. Was I upset because I had been drinking, or was the situation as serious as it felt in my heart? All I could tell her was that Jake held me down and tried to force himself on me, even though I kept telling him to stop.

Before I was able to explain how disturbed my time in his room made me feel, she quipped, "Oh yeah, that kind of thing happens all the time. I was in a guy's room just now and he tried to do the same thing." I thought to myself, is she really dismissing this type of behavior as something that is to be expected? Since when did it become the norm to be held down and touched against your will? Maybe we didn't have the same experience and if we did, we were definitely processing it differently.

As we continued to wait for the elevator, I noticed that one of my earrings was missing. It must have come out on his bed while I was jerking my head around to get away from his mouth. I loved those earrings. There were three white gold stars on each of them. They were somewhat expensive on my college budget, but there was no way I was going back to retrieve it.

I just wanted to get as far away from his room as quickly as possible. Since my concerns seemed to fall on deaf ears, I stopped trying to explain how upset I was to Kira. She just seemed to justify his behavior with a 'boys will be boys' attitude.

The sun was coming up as we walked outside. She asked if I wanted to accompany her to another football player's dorm room. They had been texting her since we all got separated to meet back up with them. I was too exhausted emotionally and physically to drive at that point, so I followed her.

We arrived at the dorm room within minutes. When we arrived everyone was going over a recap of how their night was. I declined to say anything about my night and just laid down on the edge of one of the beds. I looked out the window and watched the sunlight begin to sweep over the campus. One by one everyone fell asleep except for me.

The bed was so full of people half of my body was dangling off the side. I stared at the ceiling and listened to everyone else breathe heavily as they drifted off into sleep. Even though my body was tired, my mind was too wound-up to sleep. Replaying the night's events over and over in my head, I began to cry.

I looked around to make sure no else was awake as tears flowed down my face into my ears. As soon as they fell, I tried to wipe them away in case anyone woke up, but I couldn't catch them fast enough. There was no way I could explain why I was crying to the teammates of the guy who made me feel the way I was feeling.

Since the bed was too full for me to get comfortable and my mind wouldn't let me rest, I got up and headed to my car without waking anyone up. The meters started running at 7AM anyway, so it just made sense for me to go home and try to recover in the comfort of my own bed.

Once I got in the house, I took a shower and went to bed, but could only sleep for an hour. After tossing and turning for another hour, I decided to sit on the couch and watch TV. My mom was still resting so I sat in the living room by myself, continuing to think about what happened just a few hours earlier.

Slowly, I tried to piece things together. Did I do something to bring what happened on myself? Did I lead him on in some way? Did I overreact because I had been drinking? Although I couldn't determine how to classify what happened, I knew deep down inside something wasn't right.

From the moment I hit the couch, I couldn't stop crying. At a certain point, I turned the TV off because I couldn't see through the tears that continued to fill up my eyes. My crying was kept inaudible so I didn't alarm my mom. I didn't talk to anyone that entire day, nor did I get up other than to eat or go to the bathroom. I just sobbed in my living room by myself.

I knew I needed to get what I was feeling off my chest, and the first person I wanted to tell was my mom. I needed her love and support during the upcoming battle I was going to face if I reported what happened but it was too uncomfortable to talk about with her face-to-face. It was hard enough to admit to myself what happened, let alone try to get the words out of my mouth.

So I did what I used to do when I was younger and wanted to tell her something: I wrote her a note. It seemed like there would be less pressure if I wrote it down then tucked it in her purse for her to read at a later time. I wrote down an extremely abbreviated version of what I went through and that I had planned on reporting the incident.

When she told me she was going out to eat, the opportunity presented itself for me to make the drop. She picked up her purse, said she would be back later, and closed the door. As soon as I heard the lock click, I let out a sigh of relief.

She wouldn't see my letter until later and that would give her some time to process the information without me having to be there to witness it. Once I thought she was gone, my guard came down. With at least one person knowing, I started to feel like a weight had been lifted.

Not even two minutes later, I heard her key in the door and my heart started to race. She must have forgotten something; there was no way she saw my letter and read it already. She walked in with a stern look on her face and told me the last thing I wanted to hear: she had read my note.

She immediately started shooting questions at me. Who was the guy? What were you doing out so late? Why were you in his room alone? Were you drinking? The way she was addressing me, I began to feel what he did to me was somehow my fault. That feeling was exactly what I was trying to avoid.

As I sat there, I started to second-guess myself. Was the simple fact that I was in his room that late at night a green light for him to do whatever he wanted? I began to feel just like I did when I was 16. Helpless, taken advantage of, and disgusted with the way my body had been treated. Maybe I never should have told her, because it resulted in me being even more confused and feeling hurt all over again.

Time sort of stopped as we looked at each other for a few moments in silence. Her tone softened as she asked me more details about what happened and what I was going to do next. After I finished talking, she gave me that speech that no one wants to hear after they've been violated.

The dreaded IF speech. "Well, if you hadn't been there…If you hadn't been drinking…If you never went out that night…If you could turn back time…" There were a lot of things that night I would've done differently if given the chance, because hindsight is 20/20. My only option was to move forward the best way I could. I had to be confident in my conviction that there was nothing I did to lead him on and find strength in that.

Sexual assault was the one crime where it seemed acceptable or justified to highlight the actions of the victim leading up to the assault in order to shift blame onto them. I thought back to a short story we read in my Sociology class, about a male robbery victim. In the story, the police officer asked the victim, "Why were you walking alone so late at night? What were you wearing the night of the robbery? Why were you wearing such nice clothing as to make yourself a target? Why didn't you do more to fight back?"

The story highlighted how ridiculous the questions asked to sexual assault victims would be if asked to a victim of any other crime. Yet when someone reports being sexually assaulted, a cloud of doubt is cast over them. Sexual assault victims are often made to feel as if they did something to bring the assault on themselves. All of their choices leading up to the assault are scrutinized or judged.

After I expressed my frustration about my mom's reaction, she assured me she wasn't upset and didn't blame me. She was just trying to understand the circumstances surrounding my assault. It wasn't judgment, just concern. She asked if I wanted her to stay home with me, but I told her it was fine to go out and that I wanted to be alone. I had a lot to think about, mainly what my next step should be.

CHAPTER 6

2006

Things that I learned in my criminal justice course from the previous semester came to the front of my mind as I was sorting out how to handle what I had gone through. One of my instructors, Casey, was the head of our campus Sexual Assault Center. Since she and I interacted frequently over the course of the semester and I felt comfortable using her as a sounding board to get her advice on how to proceed.

Since what happened in Jake's room was on a Saturday night, I had to wait until Monday to speak with Casey. The first thing I did Monday morning was call and set up a time to meet with her. I didn't want to go into detail over the phone, so she told me to come in the next day.

Once I arrived, she had me sit in a small meeting room. Inside was a small metal table with four chairs around it, and a single file cabinet. There were a couple of posters on the walls, urging the reader to seek support after they've been sexually assaulted. Were they directed at me? Was I now a victim?

Casey left me alone for a few minutes while she dealt with something else, so I used that time to gather my courage to relive my experience from that weekend. After she returned, she told me to start talking as soon as I was ready about what brought me there that day. I detailed everything that happened on Saturday night from beginning to end.

I was looking for some guidance about how to classify what happened to me. I've seen what sexual assault looks like on paper or in movies, but I needed to figure out if what I experienced was a night of bad decisions or something more serious. While sitting there reliving each detail, I began to cry and my nose began to run.

There were no tissues in the room, only posters. Surely after she saw me repeatedly wiping my face with my hands, she would offer me a box of tissues. Instead, she just sat there with a straight face, focusing on every word as I continued to talk.

After I finished telling her everything about that night, she finally left to get me some tissues. She came back and told me she understood why I was so emotional and upset. Once she validated the distress I had been feeling, my tears let up. She went on to give me some options of what my next step could be.

At first, she suggested I file a police report with campus police then report it to the school administration since it happened on campus property. In my mind, Jake was a good person who simply made a drunken mistake. However, I wanted to document what he had done because I didn't want him going around thinking that type of behavior was acceptable.

I wasn't out for blood; I just wanted him to understand how his actions made me feel. I never thought I would ever have to file another report for being sexually assaulted, but I had to do everything I could to get justice for myself. If I didn't say anything and this happened to another girl, I would have felt partly to blame for allowing him to get away with what he did to me.

Before I left, Casey gave me the name of an attorney who

advocated for victims of sexual assault, specializing in college students. She didn't anticipate court being involved, but the attorney could assist me throughout the reporting process. After she told me where the campus police was located, I called them to schedule a time to file a report.

When I entered the small campus police station, there were only two employees inside. I informed them that I was there to file a report regarding a sexual assault. The man I spoke with led me to a private room to write down what happened. They told me they would follow up with me after they had gotten a statement from the witness I put down, Kira, and the person I was filing the report against, Jake.

Follow up they did not. I had to call them repeatedly to get an update on the status of my report. A few days later, they told me they would not be proceeding with my complaint because they didn't have enough evidence to file a complaint against Jake. Even though there was no physical evidence, I felt like what I told them warranted at least an investigation.

I should have filed a report with an off campus police department. As soon as I walked into their police station, I should've known they weren't going to take my report seriously. I failed to realize the challenges of trying to file a report against a football player on a college team where the athletic department made the school a lot of money.

After I got off the phone, I felt defeated. In their eyes, I didn't go through enough to get justice or any acknowledgement of what happened to me. Maybe if I hadn't gotten out of there before things got worse, there would've been enough evidence for them to charge him.

The lack of action from the campus police didn't deter my

efforts. Instead, it gave me the determination to follow through with the reporting process with the school administration and exhaust every option until there were none left. Later on that same week, Casey walked with me to the administrative offices where she had set up a meeting to file a report.

The administrator and Casey left me alone to write a detailed statement. Once I was finished, they informed me that the school's policy was to set up a meeting with the other student involved, allow them to read what I wrote, and then write their own account of what happened. I believed that when Jake saw my report, he would acknowledge what he did.

As we walked out, I thanked Casey for her support. Without her the reporting process would've been so much harder for me to handle. On my way home, I called Kira to let her know I was filing a report with the school regarding what Jake did to me. I wanted to give her a heads-up that she may be called in to show them the text messages I sent her that night and to provide any additional details.

She replied that she really didn't know anything about what happened and wasn't sure if she would be much help. Her tone was so dismissive just like the night I tried to tell her what happened outside of Jake's room. Although she wasn't in the room with us, I still expected her to offer any support she could during this extremely trying process. I hung up the phone, questioning whether she was actually my true friend.

A few days later, I got a call from Casey that Jake had made his statement to the administration and that she would accompany me to review it. Once I had seen his response, I could let the school know how I wanted to proceed. When I walked into the office, the administrator I had met with to write my statement greeted us, but her demeanor was less welcoming than the first time.

As I got to the end of Jake's statement, I was floored by his written account of that night. Of course, I wasn't expecting him to go in there and say, "I forced her to change into my clothes, held her down against her will, and tried to shove my hand up the shorts she was wearing." But after reading my statement, I was confident he would realize the magnitude of what he had done.

How naïve of me. His version of events read like a completely different evening, like he lived in an imaginary land far away from reality. None of what he said in his statement was accurate. The only thing we agreed on was that I was in his room that night.

He wrote that it was my idea to come back to his room and that I wanted to take my clothes off and get in bed with him. As far as he was concerned, I never objected to him holding me down while he tried to kiss me. At no point throughout the night had he done a single thing wrong.

He also mentioned that after the night he violated me, I had spoken to some of the guys from the football team, which was evidence that I couldn't have been too distraught. If something was really wrong then why didn't I completely cut off anyone he associated with? Since I didn't do that, it was implied that he did nothing inappropriate in his room that night.

Reading his statement crushed me. I was awake but I felt like I was stuck in a nightmare. I wanted to believe I had read it wrong but when I read it again, the lies remained the same. Not only did he violate me physically but now he was accusing me of lying about it. Prior to me going into the administrative building that day, I didn't want this to get ugly but at that moment, all I could see was red. I was determined to do whatever was necessary for my truth to be heard.

Walking out of that room after being blindsided by his words, I knew I was going to have a long and rough battle ahead of me. I didn't trust anyone anymore. Kira was becoming more and more distant. I also didn't know which guys from the football team were reporting back to Jake, so I stopped speaking to all of them.

The only person I did want to talk to about the incident with was Kevin. He was the only person on the team I thought I could trust, seeing how we knew each other before I ever stepped foot on campus. It was important for me to see if he was going to turn his back on me, as well.

I asked Kevin to meet me in his room because I needed to tell him something important. After I told him what happened, he swore he hadn't heard about it prior to me telling him. He went on to tell me that he wasn't close with Jake outside of being on the team together, so they barely spoke.

Then he made an insensitive joke, "He's such a small guy for his position. I don't understand how you couldn't get him off you." Again, I felt like I wasn't being taken seriously. I sat in silence for a minute, trying to keep it together. He saw that I wasn't amused by his comment and asked me to come sit with him on the bed.

I had no desire to be in close proximity to another male. I felt like I had lost control of my body that night, and I was hypersensitive about anyone touching me. If anyone was going to touch me again, it was going to be because I wanted them to.

Kevin could tell I was tense and made an attempt to loosen me up by kissing me on the cheek. I sat there with my eyes closed and began to cry. He wiped my tears away and held me for a few minutes. As soon as I started to feel comfortable, his hands moved from my face to the rest of my body. He kept reassuring me I was safe with him and that he would make me feel better.

The way he was touching me didn't seem like we were going slow. As I closed my eyes, I kept having flashbacks to Jake's hands and lips touching me and how disgusted I felt. My skin began to crawl but I didn't stop him.

I retreated and became numb as Kevin laid me down on the bed. As we began to have sex, I became physically nauseous. Lying there with him having sex with me, not even realizing I wasn't enjoying it or participating, made me feel empty and dirty all over again.

Tears began to fall down my face. At first, I tried to hide them, then I realized it didn't matter because he wasn't paying attention to me at all. All he cared about was climaxing. When we were done, I didn't want him to touch me a single moment longer. I just got dressed, said goodbye on the way out the door, and headed home.

When I got home, I stood in a scolding hot shower and cried like a part of me was dead. Being with someone I knew seemed like an opportunity to take back control of my body, but it ended up making me feel worse because I still wasn't having sex for me. My entire life, I had been having sex with guys because I thought that was what was expected of me. I had never found pleasure in it and never felt in control.

Walking around throughout the day, I wanted to cry all of the time. Now that Kira and I were estranged, there was no one I felt comfortable confiding in. If I came into the sorority house and someone asked me how I was doing, there was a huge lump stuck in my throat. I couldn't answer because if I did, I would want to vent about what I was going through. To avoid any emotional outburst, I ended up coming around less and less.

Not only did I drift away from my sorority sisters but I also lost any acquaintances I had on the football team. My legal advocate, Lisa, once asked me if I had considered transferring to another school as my semester was winding down. I immediately said no. It wasn't fair that I should have to leave campus and start over somewhere else when I did nothing wrong. I worked very hard to achieve excellent grades in my classes and wasn't going to risk losing credits by transferring to another school.

As the weeks went by, it became clear why she made that suggestion. During the reporting and investigation process, I was still working, attending 18 credits worth of classes, and preparing for finals. One afternoon, while sitting in the third row of my Drugs and Crime lecture, I began to cry uncontrollably.

I was emotionally and mentally overwhelmed. Everything about that night kept replaying in my mind, and the feeling of repulsion moved from my gut to my chest and into my throat. I gathered my things, quietly exited the lecture, and cried in a bathroom stall until it was time for my next class.

Being on campus would bring on anxiety. I never knew who was aware of what I was going through. Whenever anyone looked at me longer than a glance or smirked in my direction, I thought they were judging me. It felt like everyone was talking about me behind my back, which led to feelings of paranoia, isolation, and depression.

It got so bad that when I saw any of the football players or their girlfriends, I feared they would verbally attack me as I walked by. During half-time at one of the school basketball games, some of my sorority sisters and I were sitting in our usual front row seats when a group of cheerleaders passed in front of us. There was nothing unusual about that until they stopped directly in front of me.

One of the black female cheerleaders stepped forward and asked, "Are you the bitch who was hanging around with my boyfriend?" At first, I thought it was a joke, but the look on her face showed me she wasn't kidding. It was like watching a scene out of a movie.

I denied knowing what she was talking about, but she insisted she knew it was me and if I ever said anything to her boyfriend again, she would "beat my ass". After the group of cheerleaders walked away, I looked around and everyone seated near me was staring at me.

Her boyfriend was one of the biggest jerks on the football team, but he was a part of the group I was hanging with before going to Jake's room. After I reported Jake to the school, he did everything in his power to make my life a living hell. I'm sure her boyfriend put something in her ear to make her confront me just to torment me even further.

Prior to that incident, it came to my attention that her boyfriend, along with other guys on the team, had solicited their friends from outside of school to approach me if they saw me out. Their mission was to get me to have sex with them. When that wasn't successful, the players resorted to telling people that I was a slut with a variety of STDs. They even spread around a long, yet inaccurate, list of guys I had slept with.

I spent the rest of my semester alone. If I wasn't in class or at work, I stayed at home. My interest in the sorority declined to the point where I would make up excuses for not being able to attend the activities we were hosting. I didn't want to go to any more sporting events because I didn't want that seen as indication that I was supporting the athletes. I finished the semester with an A in all of my classes, but everything else about my life was crumbling around me.

Over the summer, I did a reassessment of how I spent my time and who I spent it with. At the beginning of the next semester, I ended up dropping out of the sorority. It was too much for me to handle with 18 credits worth of classes while working part-time and commuting back and forth. With the lack of support I got from my sorority sisters, being there wasn't worth the time commitment.

Coincidentally, the only two other minority females in the sorority left at the same time I did. I had no clue they were leaving when I made my decision, but they both felt the same way I did. We didn't feel the bond expected from being a part of a sorority, and some of the sisters outright made us feel unwelcome.

During the first few weeks of classes, I got a call from the school administration to set up a meeting. They didn't give me details about what was going on, but they did tell me a decision had not been reached regarding my complaint against Jake. I contacted Casey to attend the meeting with me but since she had a prior engagement, she sent one of the other advocates in her place.

When I arrived, the administration office informed me that they had anonymously received a photo of me in relation to my complaint against Jake. The woman handed me a print-out of an old picture from my Myspace page. In it, I'm wearing only a bikini bottom and a blazer that was covering my breast.

The only skin you could see were my stomach and legs. Regardless, whoever sent the photo was trying to depict me as a half-naked slut who paraded around on the internet exploiting myself. Even if that were the case, it didn't make what Jake did to me any less real or wrong.

I couldn't believe how low the people from his side would go to slander my character in order to defend him. My advocate asked the woman from the administration office what that picture had to do with what happened on the night in question. She demanded that the school divulge who sent the picture, and she wanted that person reprimanded.

A few days later, Casey notified me that one of the coaches from the football team sent the photo. I was disgusted and refused to attend or support any of my school's athletic events from that point forward. Heading to the stadium early for every home game to get front row seats was a thing of the past. The fact that an employee of the school went to such lengths to intimidate and degrade a female student filing a sexual assault report was inexcusable. These attacks didn't make it any easier to manage my depression and anxiety. Being emotionally and mentally broken with a dwindling list of friends, I needed to seek help to cope with the drastic changes and continuous battles I faced.

The only positive resource left at school was the health center. Not only could students receive health care for free and prescriptions at a low cost, but they also offered mental health services. Casey referred me to a school psychologist, Jaime, who she thought would be a good fit for me.

The school only allotted a certain amount of complimentary visits with a psychologist, so I made sure to take advantage of every one of them. At first, it was hard to tell a stranger the ins and outs of my life but in order for our sessions to be effective, I couldn't hold back the things I would hide from anyone else. Initially, I resented her for pointing out all of the poor choices I had made, but that's what she was there for—to give me an honest, unfiltered, unbiased opinion.

When I started, I thought our sessions would only focus on

what happened to me on campus. Instead, we ended up delving into issues ranging from the effect my father had on me to my history of unhealthy and one-sided relationships with men. She helped me recognize that all of my relationships with the opposite sex had been unhealthy in some way.

My father came in my life when I was about ten years old then made the decision to not be an active parent. Ever since that perceived rejection, I searched for a man to fill that void. Even though I had nothing positive to say about my father, I always ended up with men who were just like him. Unsupportive, bad boy image, verbally abusive, poor at communication and emotionally unavailable. The list went on and on.

Once a week, Jaime would help me address all of the issues I needed to work on, the signs I refused to see, and what changes I could make within myself to foster healthier relationships. She became my only confidant for quite some time. Her office was a safe place that I looked forward to going to.

One afternoon, she made a poignant revelation that would change the choices I made forever. While working on my trust issues and poor choices, we began to sort through why I was constantly getting into relationships I knew were unhealthy and unfulfilling. I always wanted to believe in the good in people, even if they repeatedly let me down. I had become accustomed to accepting the very least from others in the hopes that my loyalty and persistence would eventually be rewarded.

As we were talking about my relationships with Curt, Kevin, and the guys who came before them, a pattern began to present itself. The guys I threw all of my time and energy into throughout my teens were always the ones who would disappear and were hard to reach. The less attention they paid to me, the more I would do to get it. Any morsel of affection from them would refuel my desire, no matter how many times they let me down or abandoned me.

She described my behavior in such a way that it spoke to my core and gave me the wakeup call I needed. "Think of what you've been doing this way. You say these guys don't call you or spend time with you consistently, yet you still hang around, waiting for them to change. You hope that one day, miraculously, their actions will be different."

She went on to say, "It's like you're telling them, 'I'm hungry' and their response is to give you the crumbs from a sandwich. That's not going to fill you up, it will never fill you up, but you still accept it instead of going out and finding someone who would give you an entire sandwich to make you full."

In a million years, I would have never thought of what I was doing that way, but she was absolutely right. It made perfect sense; if I continued investing time in men who were never going to fulfil my needs or wants, I would always be left feeling empty. No matter what excuses these guys gave me for the way they treated me, my patience and forgiveness was never going to result in the healthy relationship I desired.

The happy ending I envisioned for myself was never going to be attainable if I continued to accept nothing but the bare minimum. I needed to hold men to a higher standard and not just hold onto the scraps they would throw at me to keep me on the hook. My desire was to be full, and I needed to make better choices in order to get there.

Going to therapy and getting some of my confidence back with a new sense of awareness gave me the boost I needed to fight for a resolution regarding my complaint against Jake. No matter what anyone said about me or how anyone tried to bully me, I wasn't going to waver. They could try to break me, but I wasn't going to back down or go away.

As my senior year was coming to an end, Casey called one afternoon to inform me that the school had finally finished their investigation after several months. Jake had finally taken responsibility for what he did to me the year before. As a part of his penalty, he had to write me an apology letter, he would no longer be able to live in campus housing, and he was required to take a sexual assault prevention course and participate in community service.

After finding out he was going to be held accountable for the physical and emotional pain he inflicted on me, I sighed with relief. I finally felt like the school cared and took the safety of their students seriously. Although it seemed like an eternity later and I went through so much to get it, there was restitution and validation for my assault.

In his letter, he apologized for how he made me feel that night in his room. At the time, he didn't realize how his actions impacted me but over time, the magnitude of what he did became clear. He was truly remorseful because he would never want anything like that to happen to his mother or his sister. The letter was hard to believe after reading the original statement he wrote when I first reported him to the school. This time, it felt like words coming from a human being with feelings as opposed to the spineless coward I saw him as over the previous year.

It felt like a weight had been lifted off of me and I could enjoy a positive experience just as my time on campus was coming to an end. That was until I picked up a copy of the campus newspaper in the Student Union a few days later. While making my way to the Sudoku puzzle in the back, I stumbled upon a featured piece in the paper with Jake's name in the headline.

In the article, it mentioned the off-campus apartment he had been residing in prior to deciding that he was leaving school to enter the NFL draft. It went on to say how proud the school was of his achievements, both on and off the field. By the end of the article, the school's song and dance about how sternly they had disciplined him for assaulting me was out the window.

What was the school so proud of off the field? They covered up the fact that he sexually assaulted me and were now singing his praises. That he was a lying, vindictive, controlling chauvinist? How could he lose campus housing if he wasn't currently living on campus? Was he actually assigned any community service? Everything they told me appeared to be a lie; even the authenticity of his 'apology' letter was in question.

My first phone call was to Casey to inform her of everything that was in the article. She told me she was going to immediately question the administration on the validity of his punishments. After several phone calls, no one from the school ever got back to her regarding his sanctions.

I was done. What was the point? If the administration would lie to make me feel as if I received some sort of retribution then I was fighting a losing battle. The only positive things I could take away from attending that school was my education and the lessons I learned in therapy.

Once my one-on-one sessions ran out with Jaime, she suggested I attend group therapy for sexual assault victims on campus. She and another therapist, Lauren, facilitated the group. The first session consisted of seven female students. Each of us attended every week and shared our sexual assault experiences, as well as the challenges of healing while, in some cases, attending the same school as our attackers.

I was relieved to finally have a sense of comradery after feeling completely alone and abandoned on campus for so long. With the way I was being treated by the school administration, campus police, the football team and its staff as well as some of the students, I'd felt like the only person who ever reported a sexual assault on campus.

After meeting and talking with the support group for weeks, the time came for the annual Clothesline Project to be displayed on campus. The Clothesline Project was a way for victims of sexual assault or domestic violence, and friends and family affected by it, to express themselves by putting their thoughts or feelings onto a t-shirt. Those shirts were then displayed all over campus for a week.

Everyone in the group was nervous about publicly expressing their own personal experience, but the therapists assured us it would be therapeutic and anonymous. I debated long and hard about what I wanted to put on my shirt. I wanted to blast the school, Jake, the football team, Kira—anyone who hurt me, no matter how large or small. Then I thought about what would happen if someone saw it and figured out I made it. Would I receive backlash all over again?

Eventually, I made a decision about what my t-shirt would say. I had spent so long being ostracized and isolated that the only person whose opinion truly mattered about what my shirt said was me. I was no longer afraid of standing up and letting people know how the school and athletic department handled accusations of misconduct by an athlete.

All of the girls stood in the therapy room quietly, using the material provided to make their shirts. Mine was blue. On the front, I painted a large football and wrote in capitalized black letters on the back: "A football player assaulted me on campus. The football staff and players bullied me. The school administration lied about punishing him. Making money off football games is more important than students' safety."

As I walked to class the next week, I nervously headed towards the Clothesline Project displays. I was overwhelmed by the number of shirts that were hung around campus. While reading the shirts, I was saddened by the magnitude of how many people had been affected by sexual assault and domestic violence. The majority of the student body probably had no idea how many people had been victimized on campus. I didn't know until I saw how many shirts were hanging.

I finally spotted the blue t-shirt I had created and realized a trend in the shirts surrounding it as I got closer. The organizers had put all of the t-shirts related to school athletes together. Surprisingly, other girls were a lot bolder than I was and wrote the names and jersey numbers of the players who had assaulted them. A lot of names I recognized, and some of them I had hung out with before. One shirt was a replica of an alumni's NFL jersey with the word 'RAPIST' in bold red paint written over his name.

I had never heard about any of these assaults—not on the local news, not in an article in our school newspaper, not even on campus. Some of those guys were still on campus, walking around like they had never done a single thing wrong in their lives. These women's stories were swept under the rug while the players who violated them in some way were continuously praised. None of the players named on those shirts ever seemed to face any consequences for allegedly assaulting someone. Instead their names were plastered in lights and they were given accolades and special treatment.

Most of them were either thriving as football players on our university's team or in the NFL. While I was sick to my stomach about the fact that none of these victims appeared to receive justice for what they had been through, at least I wasn't alone in feeling let down and frustrated. It appeared that the school covering up sexual assaults by their star football players had been going on long before I got there.

I wondered how many of the girls who made those shirts reported their assault to the school. Out of those assaults reported, how many times had the school covered it up to save face and keep the money machine that was our athletics department running smoothly? Having a scandal come out about a football player would've been too detrimental, so why not just shut the complainant up with false promises?

When I walked around campus and someone looked at me too long, I was no longer afraid they knew my story. I no longer felt guilty about reporting Jake, because I had done nothing wrong. The school was wrong, the coaches on the football team were wrong, the campus police was wrong. They were the ones covering up assaults on campus by student athletes. If only those were the stats handed out in the school's welcome packet.

Only a few months out of college, I was hired at a prestigious government contracting company that provided me with the opportunity to travel all over the U.S. However, my first year was spent behind a desk. From the moment I got in I answered

CHAPTER 7

2007

phone calls and responded to emails or letters that were addressed to various government agencies. Our job was to be the middle man between the public and the government officials they were trying to reach.

While there were many requests from students seeking resources for school assignments, there were also victims of crime that would reach out seeking justice or assistance. There was also a lot of correspondence in support of legalizing drugs. Most of the handwritten letters came from people in jail claiming they were innocent and pleading to have the government to investigate their wrongful conviction. My favorite reading materials were the occasional claims that the government implanted tracking devices in their homes or in their body and they wanted them removed.

One of the upsides of working for an agency that contracted with the government meant we got holidays off. Sitting at my desk on New Year's Eve, I was constantly checking the clock, hoping my manager would come by and tell me I could leave early, which usually happened the day before a holiday. Since I couldn't focus on work, I started checking social media on my phone when a phone call from Emily came in.

She and I had met in group therapy but hadn't hung out much since I graduated. After a bit of catching up, she asked if I had any plans that night. When I said no, she asked if I wanted to make an easy 150 dollars. Her boyfriend's club needed someone to run the coat check for the night. Since they were expecting a large turnout for the holiday, there was no way they could go without a coat check attendant.

I mulled it over for a few minutes and decided why not make a few extra dollars. My only alternative was to sit by myself at home while eating ice cream and watching a *Sex and the City* marathon. She gave me the details and asked me to be there by 9 PM.

After running home and changing into something more festive, I headed to Poise Bar, located in the Adams Morgan area of DC. I had never been there before, but it was one of the more popular clubs on the strip. Emily's boyfriend greeted me at the door and showed me to the small coat check room by the stairs on the second floor. He showed me where everything was and left me to organize the hangers and tickets.

As the first few guests began to arrive, everything was running smoothly. I had gotten into a groove of hanging coats and handing out claim tickets. When the club began to get crowded, that resulted in the coat check filling up. Very quickly, I began to run out of space. While trying to squeeze every coat I could on the rack, some coats began to fall off of the hangers and I couldn't tell which number the coat corresponded to.

I was getting overwhelmed and there was no more space for jackets so I began to turn people away. As soon a told the first skinny blonde in a Forever 21 dress that I couldn't take her coat, she began to scream at me about how ridiculous that was. After the fifteenth person berated me for not having space for their coat, I radioed for someone who worked there to come help me.

A manager came over and tried to calm me down. He said there was nothing I could do about the coat check being full and to let people know it was closed until more space became available then shut the door. As soon as he left, I sat in there with the lights off, hiding from the dozens of people who kept knocking on the door. As soon as someone came to retrieve their coat, there was always someone behind them ready to take their hanger.

Never in a million years did I think one night of coat check would be so intense and stressful. As people began to leave after the ball dropped, the amount of coats went down and I was finally able to breathe. It took a while to sort out the coats that had fallen off the hangers but other than that, the night was getting much better.

From across the room, I saw a guy staring at me as he was coming down the stairs. I hoped he wasn't looking because of how disheveled I appeared. He made his way across the room and propped his arm up on the door of the coat check with confidence. He introduced himself as Blake, the more he talked, I could tell he was a bit cocky and a jokester. At first, I thought he was too aggressive, but the fact that he made me laugh offset how over-the-top he was.

After he wore me down enough to give him my number, he made a strange comment about his accessories. On his wrist was a bracelet with dozens of jewels that he confessed was fake. "You see this bracelet? It's not real but I have one just like it that is real. I'm not going to wear my real stuff out, those are just for me."

I found his statement to be extremely odd and unnecessary. Who buys real diamonds but wears fake diamonds for special occasions? And what was the point of telling me? The little bit of charm he exhibited at first was wearing off.

At that point, it was too late to take my number back, so I just laughed nervously and told him to enjoy the rest of his night. Around 3 AM, I was finally done with coat check and walked away with a little over two hundred dollars. I was exhausted and couldn't wait to get home and go to bed.

As I was walking to my car, a strange number popped up on my phone. When I answered, Blake was on the other end asking if I wanted to come hang out with him at his friend's house. There was no way he was being serious. We had just met an hour ago, but he thought getting together at 3 o'clock in the morning was an ideal first date. Maybe he was drunk or really feeling himself, but either way he was inappropriate.

I told him there was no way I was going to meet him that late at night but we could make plans to do something at a decent hour and hung up. Later on that day, he called me to ask if I wanted to go see a movie. One of my favorite activities was going to the movies, so I agreed. When I asked which one so I could look up movie times, he had no idea which movies were playing.

We went back and forth for over ten minutes trying to figure out what to see. We were getting nowhere, so I decided to axe the movie idea altogether and suggested dinner instead. When it came to food, he was very decisive. He wanted Chipotle.

Chipotle, no matter how scrumptious their burrito bowls were, was not a first date destination. His recommendation threw me off so much I told him I would call him back and hung up abruptly. With my mom being my best friend, I went to her for even the smallest decision making assistance.

I called her into the living room to ask if I should suck it up and go to a semi-fast food restaurant with this guy or sit at home and save myself the trouble. She replied, "Hey, it's a free meal. You might as well go, maybe it won't be that bad."

Begrudgingly, I called him back, asking if Chipotle was even going to be open since it was a holiday. He assured me it would be. So I asked which one he wanted to meet at, to which he responded, "Well, actually right now I don't have a car, so if you pick me up I'll direct you to the one near my mom's house."

At that moment, I had to put the phone down to reassess my life choices. Did he really just say pick him up, to head to a fast food place? It was like being in high school all over again.

Since I had already agreed to meet him, I just told him to text me the address and got off the phone. As I was getting dressed, with each item of clothing I put on I wanted to take it right back off and text him that I was no longer coming. As I got in my car and put his address in my GPS, I mentally prepared myself for what was sure to be a miserable date.

The first thing he did when he got into my car was present me with his rap CD, which looked like a bootleg disc, and encouraged me to listen to it. Instead of going with my initial reaction to throw it out the window while driving, I just tossed it in the back seat when he wasn't looking.

I was so upset with myself for even giving this loser my phone number I barely spoke the entire ride. I was never good at hiding my feelings so if I spoke, it was going to be with an attitude. Saying as little as possible was the best thing for both of us as I patiently followed his turn-by-turn directions to the Chipotle near his mom's house.

On the ride there, he told me how he was staying on his mom's couch while working on his rapping career. The more he talked, the more I wanted to reach across his body, open the door, and push him out of my car. Nothing he said made me want to continue being in his presence.

After about 10 minutes, we arrived in the downtown area of Silver Spring where there were plenty of eateries to choose from that weren't fast food. As I drove past the Chipotle, it was completely dark. Like I thought, it was closed for New Year's Day. Instead of just parking and going to another restaurant, he said, "No worries; I have another spot we can go to that will be perfect."

Once again, I remained completely silent except to ask which turn I needed to take next. For another 10 minutes, I listened to him talk about his rap career. When he asked me why I wasn't talking, I simply told him my throat was sore without even glancing in his direction. The evening couldn't get any worse, or so I thought.

"Make a right at the light. Then take a left here. Now turn into this shopping center." When he told me to park the car, I realized he had given me directions to a Popeye's. That is Popeye's Louisiana Kitchen specializing in fast food fried chicken and biscuits. In order to keep myself from bursting into tears, I had to laugh at how this night was turning out.

My mom's advice was definitely the wrong call in this case. Before getting out, he asked if he could smoke in my car. Before I could catch myself, I barked at him, "Why would you think you can smoke in my car if I don't smoke?" Without saying anything, he got out to light up while I stayed inside the car.

Should I just pull off and leave him to find his own way home? I didn't have it in me to do that, so instead I set in motion my plan to escape. I called my mom and explained to her the terrible mistake I had made by going out with this clown. I instructed her that in 5 minutes she was to call me and make up some emergency, giving me an excuse to leave.

Since this guy was bringing me to Popeye's, I was just going to pay for my own food and box it up to go. As I pulled out my wallet, he popped up from behind me and placed his order with the cashier. Then he turned to me with a grin and said, "I've got it this time, but next time is on you, right?"

There was no way I could respond without biting his head off, so I just ignored his comment and stepped to the side to wait for my food. It seemed like those 5 minutes were dragging along. He picked up the tray containing our food and asked where I wanted to sit, as if we were choosing between a booth in the back or a table with a view at a fine dining restaurant. I thought to myself, does it really matter where we sit because all of the chairs are plastic.

Finally, my phone rang and there was an end in sight to first date for dummies. My mom was on the other end, vying for 'Best Performance Resulting in the End of a Date' as if Blake could hear her talking. In this scene, she was locked out of the house, sitting in her car in the dead of winter, and needing me to come back and let her in. In actuality, she was calling from the comfort of her friend's couch.

After informing Blake that I needed to leave to rescue my mom from being stranded in the cold, his response was, "Should I finish eating first?" I couldn't believe this guy was so clueless about all things in life. Once again, I bit my tongue and went back to the counter to grab to-go containers and instructed him that we needed to go not now, but right now.

There was no way I could've gotten him back to his mom's apartment any faster. I may have even pulled away before he finished closing the car door. Dates like that were the exact reason why I didn't mind being single. I would rather sit at home by myself than endure an evening with a guy who had no clue how to court a woman.

My experience with Blake inspired my first blog. I had never been interested in blogging before, but I just couldn't keep that experience to myself. After I shared the link on my Facebook profile, I got a bunch of sympathy from women who had been on similar horrific dates and shocked responses from men who couldn't believe this guy's audacity. While going through that experience, it wasn't funny but when I told the story, other people found it to be hilarious.

Blake tried calling me and texting me a few times after our fried chicken rendezvous, but I didn't respond. One day, he sent me a disrespectful message about me ignoring him, so I simply sent him the link to the blog I wrote about our date. He was livid.

He blew my phone up with a series of text messages with "Do you know who I am?" "Google me!" "Screw you!" They went on and on and were so profane that I didn't need to read all of them to get the gist of what he was saying.

Since I had nothing to focus on but work, I began to exceed my manager's expectations and received multiple accolades. Shortly after my first year, I was promoted to a position where I was given more responsibilities and tasked with training new employees.

My new role included exhibiting and presenting materials at conferences across the country. I traveled to each event by myself and spent my downtime exploring each city. Other people in my office had spouses, kids, or significant others at home, so they turned down many of the traveling assignments. I had none of those so I volunteered to travel anywhere at any time.

Some of my most enjoyable trips were when I traveled by myself. One of my favorite places to vacation solo was Miami. The first thing I would do after checking into my hotel was walk down Ocean Drive, grab a drink, and people-watch. The best time to go was in the afternoon when it was warm and sunny, because there were men working out on the beach shirtless.

I would sip my frozen strawberry daiquiri, sit on the brick wall along the beach and shamelessly watch them flex and sweat. After getting a little tipsy, I would go back to my room and take a nap. My entire trip would be spent eating, sleeping, shopping, or exploring.

Unfortunately, none of my conferences were held in Miami, but work allowed me to see other parts of the U.S. I never would have visited for pleasure. While on a business trip in Huntsville, Alabama, I met a tall, dark, and handsome guy named Jeff. Huntsville was the last place on earth I would ever expect to meet an attractive black man my age.

At the conference center where my event was being held, there was a semi-pro football team that would attend practice on the same level as my exhibit. Each day, the players would walk by, staring at me and whispering amongst themselves. Jeff was the only one who stopped and spoke to me.

We tried to get together on my first night there, but neither of us had a vehicle to get around in. Since he was new to the city, he didn't have tags for his truck yet and my job wouldn't reimburse me for taking a cab outside of a certain area for leisure. If he wasn't going to come get me, I wasn't going to pay out of my pocket to see him.

On my last night in Huntsville, Jeff was finally able to pick me up for dinner. I invited him inside the hotel to grab some complimentary finger food and drinks being offered to guests staying there for business. On the way downstairs in the elevator, he surprised me with a kiss that was knee-buckling. It almost made me want to push the button for my floor instead of the lobby.

When we weren't kissing, we were talking nonstop about everything from our families to where we saw ourselves in 5 years. At the restaurant, he was so respectful that I felt like I was on my first real grown-up date. We sat next to each other in the booth flirting, drinking cocktails, and staring into each other's eyes the entire night.

Once we got back to my room, we sat around for a while, continuing to learn more about each other and gradually getting more comfortable on the bed. Then he began to undress me, kissing his way down my body. I hadn't been intimate with anyone since college and I was extremely nervous.

After leaving school, I had no desire for casual sex. Sex had never been enjoyable or fulfilling for me. The entire time, I just laid there, feeling like I was simply a vessel for a guy to get his rocks off. My view of sex was tainted and unless I was completely comfortable, I didn't want to do it.

When it came time for us to have sex, my mind was racing. What if I ended up being disappointed or feeling used again? What if I had another flashback and started crying? I didn't want him to end the night thinking I was crazy.

Luckily for me, Jeff was the opposite of what I had experienced in the past, and it was exactly what I needed. He wasn't one-dimensional like all of the other guys I had been with. His goal wasn't just to have sex and leave. He actually found pleasure in pleasuring me.

Before that night, I had never been a fan of oral sex. Guys would claim their oral skills would change my life but in the end, they would put me to sleep. Jeff took oral sex to the next level. I had never felt so much pleasure before, especially not just from a guy going down on me.

My entire body became warm, and I couldn't control the shaking in my legs. That was the first time I not only enjoyed oral sex but I also didn't have to fake an orgasm. After he was finished, he didn't pressure me to reciprocate like guys had done in the past.

When it came time to have sex, he took everything slowly. I never thought I would encounter a man who could bring me to a place of euphoria like he did. His arms were so strong he would pick me up and place me where he wanted me. I didn't feel like he was taking advantage of me; instead, it felt like he was taking care of me.

We spent hours rolling around, knocking pillows off the bed and kicking lamps over in my hotel room. By the time the sun came up, the sheets were strewn across the room. We were both covered in sweat and panting from exhaustion. I'm sure my hair was all over my head and partially stuck to my face, but I didn't even care; everything about that night was amazing.

Jeff revitalized me sexually after spending so much time closed-off. I left Huntsville and went back to my life in Maryland feeling like an awakened version of myself. Sex didn't have power over me anymore, and it didn't have to be an uncomfortable experience. I just had to make sure that any man I chose to be intimate with wanted the experience to be enjoyable for the both of us.

When I arrived at the airport, my mom was there to pick me up, as she frequently did whenever I took a trip. On the ride home, she was acting strange, being very quiet and not making eye contact. A few minutes into the drive, she nervously stated that she had something to tell me.

I figured she was going to say that she accidentally deleted one of my TV shows off the DVR or something. Her such a dramatic build-up seemed unnecessary. I urged her to spit it out because the suspense was making me nervous.

She started by mentioning that she had searched for my half-brothers' names to see what was going on with them. She discovered that my oldest brother was in prison after being convicted of some pretty serious charges. He was found guilty of felony murder after shooting a man while trying to rob him.

I was so grateful to have avoided that kind of lifestyle. It seemed like generation after generation on my father's side of the family was involved with drugs, violent crime, and ultimately faced jail time. Then there was another long pause in the conversation and I thought that was all of the news she had to share.

While sitting at a red light, my mom told me she had also done a search of my father's name. I was waiting for her to tell me he was locked up right next to his son. It had been years since I heard from him, so I was hoping that was his excuse for not maintaining a relationship with his only daughter. I looked over at her and I could tell what she had to say was weighing on her.

I turned the radio down and encouraged her to go on. She finally spoke. "Your father passed away." I sat back and let her words sank in. I didn't feel the need to cry, which I felt guilty about. I was confused about how I was feeling and how to react.

Since I didn't respond, my mom continued, "I Googled his name and the first result was his obituary from when he died in October." We were currently in February of the following year. My first definitive emotion rose to the surface.

I skipped over the grief stage and went right to anger. Even though my father and I weren't close, not a single person from his side of the family reached out to me or my mom to notify us he had passed away. I was never going to be able to pay my respects at his funeral. His family robbed me of seeing him put to rest and saying goodbye.

I still hadn't spoken, so my mom asked what was going through my mind. The only thought I could formulate was how messed up it was she had to find out about his death by Googling him. Then I had to face the fact that I would never be able to repair our relationship.

Even though I was the child, maybe I should've been the bigger person and reached out to him. It hurt me that he was always so close with his sons but he never seemed to want to keep in touch with me. He would always call my mother to try to see her but would never ask to see or speak to me.

He missed the majority of my birthdays, my first bike ride with my training wheels off, my miscarriage, my prom, both high school and college graduations, my first heartbreak, and every other milestone in my life. The few years he was in and out of my life were spent making things more difficult for me and my mom. The only memories I had of him were filled with resentment, fear, and anger—no positive memories whatsoever.

Many make the mistake of thinking that there's all the time in the world to repair relationships with people. They just keep putting it off until the next day, and when that day passes they promise to do it the next week. When there's a falling out or an argument, you take for granted that there will be another opportunity to apologize and make things right.

I wish I had time to explain to my father how he hurt me. How abandoned I felt not only from him being absent from my childhood but also when he didn't take full advantage of being able to come back into my life. How all of my poor choices regarding the men in my past stemmed from my broken relationship with him.

My first interaction with my father was when I was 10 years old. The last time I saw him was when I was 17. He died when I was 22. Cumulatively, he only spent about two years active in my life. He made a small cameo in the story of my life. The purpose of his storyline was to ruin every expectation I had of having a loving father and to show me how reckless, selfish, and hurtful men could be.

As soon as I got home, I went online to look for his obituary. Once I found it and started reading, my heart dropped in my chest. In his obituary, where it listed who he was 'survived by', his sons were proudly listed but there was no mention of me, his oldest child and only daughter. Having him as a father felt the same as my mother picking a random donor at a sperm bank.

When he was alive, his family made me feel like an outsider, as if I didn't belong. Even after his passing, they continued to make me feel as if I meant nothing to them. Before I knew him, I had built up an ideal of who my father was and wanted him to be a part of my life. At that moment, I wondered if I would have been better off never meeting him. According to the final summarization of his life, I didn't exist anyway.

Dealing with his death and his impact on my life forced me to face the fact that I was carrying around a lot of anger and pain. The obituary was the final gut punch to motivate me to address the feelings of unworthiness and abandonment that I was holding onto. Feelings I realized I had been taking out on everyone else but him.

Now that I would never be able to address the root of my issues with the man who started them, I had to let go in order to move on. It wasn't healthy for me to let it fester any longer. I needed to let go of the rejection I felt from my own father and stop internalizing that to mean I was never going to be good enough for anyone who wanted to treat me right.

I made the conscious decision to take what Jaime taught me in therapy and move forward with my life. It wasn't going to be a quick fix, but I was willing to let go of the unhealthy way I saw myself because of my father and start on to the long road towards healthier relationships with not only other people, but most importantly myself. I was going to start with valuing myself more and holding the people I let into my life to a higher standard.

After finding out all I could online about my father's death, I reached out to my half-brothers. The youngest never responded. My mom spoke with his grandmother and found out he was having an extremely difficult time handling our father's death. He was a spitting image of him and every time he looked in the mirror, he saw his face.

Since the older one was in prison, I looked up his inmate number and location through the Maryland Correctional Services website. I didn't know how he would receive me reaching out to him, so I started out with a brief letter. Within a few weeks, he wrote me back and sent some photos.

He also was having a hard time and was upset about not

being able to attend the funeral. As I read that I thought to myself, at least he was notified about it. We sent several letters back and forth over a few months. Prior to being arrested, he had a daughter and also sent me pictures of her from when she came to visit him in prison.

Eventually, he added my name to his visiting list and welcomed me to come on his designated visiting days. Since I hadn't seen him in years, and he mentioned that he didn't get a lot of visitors, my mom and I took the two-hour drive together to go see him. When we arrived, they wouldn't let my mom in the visitor's area because she wasn't on his list.

She insisted I go in without her and that she would sit in the car and wait for me. I went through the metal detectors and walked back into a large open room with a long, u-shaped table with several bank teller-like openings at each seat. There were many pairs seated already, conducting their visits.

As I walked to my seat assigned by the corrections officer, the inmates on the other side of the partition followed me with their eyes. After a few minutes, I saw someone walk out who looked like a much older and worn down version of the brother I remembered. He was missing several teeth, had gained a good amount of weight, and had a body full of tattoos.

It felt strange sitting across from him at first. The memories I had of him weren't fond ones but if there was a time to forgive him and move on, it was in that moment. We sat there for our hour-long visit talking mostly about how my life had been going since his life only consisted of being in prison. He briefly discussed the circumstances about his arrest but mainly talked about his pride and joy, his daughter.

After our hour was up, I gave him a hug under watch from

the guards and told him I would make time to visit him again. Eventually, life got in the way and I did a poor job of expediently responding to his letters. When I moved the next year, I sent him a letter to notify him of my new address.

He never wrote me another letter after I moved. I also never made it back to visit him. Maybe I reminded him too much of what he was missing. Maybe he reminded me too much of the path my life could've taken had my father had a bigger influence in my life. Either way, our lives continued the way they always had: separately.

CHAPTER 8

2009

I kept the fact that my father passed away to myself. I hadn't talked much about him before I found out about his death, so I didn't feel the need to bring him up after. When it did come up, everyone would respond with "I'm so sorry for your loss." I wanted to respond that you couldn't lose something you never had.

While gradually working through the issues I had with my father, I felt myself becoming lighter and more positive. The negativity I used to carry around, was getting less powerful. My goal was to not let my daddy issues turn me into a bitter black woman, skeptical of every man who came into my life.

I worked on being open and optimistic about starting relationships. Every situation was approached with a new mindset. Anyone I encountered was treated as an individual. I had to stop assuming everyone was going to disappoint me or let me down before they actually did.

The characteristics I desired in a man also changed. Learning more about myself clarified the qualities a man needed to possess in order to complement what I had to offer. Instead of shutting men down because they didn't come in the perfect package, I was open to giving guys that weren't my usual type a chance. No more unrealistic expectations or trying to nab the most attractive guy in the room. I needed less flash and more stability.

While out with my friends, I would mingle to see what was out there. When that was unsuccessful I tried my hand at online dating. After filtering through the guys who were trolling the internet for hookups, I went on a couple of dates. Shortly after the dates began, I realized why those particular guys were looking for love online. They were socially awkward and struggled to make conversation. I was pretty outgoing and confident so that method of finding dates didn't suit me. On top of that, their online photos were usually more flattering than how they looked in real life.

After a string of disastrous dates, my coworker Amy and I decided to grab dinner one night at Lucky Strikes to take our minds off our disappointing romantic lives. Since I wasn't feeling well, I threw on a plaid shirt and ill-fitting jeans before heading out that night. I had no makeup on and my hair tied back into a ponytail. I left the house not really caring what I looked like since I had just planned on having a low-key evening.

She had met some guys from a motorcycle crew who invited her to a block party for people with bikes. She asked me to tag along. We pulled up the address that the guy gave her and it was in a part of DC that we had never been to before. When we arrive the street was empty. A block party wasn't really something you could miss. Either the guy was playing her or the event was cancelled. We had drove all the way out to DC so we decided to grab something to eat to keep the night going.

Unfortunately, we encountered some of the worst service of our lives that night. I had worked in the service industry for years, so my standards were already lower than most because I knew how challenging serving was. For me to classify someone's service as horrible was a mighty feat.

I was coming down with a cold, so the first thing I asked for was a hot tea. The waitress told me they didn't serve hot tea. I smiled at her and explained to her that my throat was killing me, so if there was any way I could get just hot water with lemon it would be greatly appreciated. In my experience, I would commonly tell guest we didn't have hot drinks simply because it was inconvenient to prepare, so I hoped telling her I was ill would help my case.

After she took our food order, she disappeared into the back. Several minutes later, a man brought me a cup of hot water, a tea bag, and lemon. Victory was mine. As I finished my first cup of tea, Amy and I paused our conversation long enough to realize we hadn't seen our server since she took our initial order.

Every time we needed a new drink, utensils, or more food, we had to go to the bar. Even when our food came out, there was no sign of her. As we continued to talk and laugh, we tried to keep the poor service from bothering us.

Just as we were complaining about men and how hard dating was for both of us, three men sat down at the table next to us. Out of habit, I gave each of them the full head-to-toe assessment. There was a bald, dark-skinned guy of average height, a short Hispanic guy with gelled-back, black hair, and a light-skinned, bald guy who stood about 6 feet tall. Immediately, I determined I wasn't interested in any of them.

As Amy and I talked a little more, I glanced back over at the table of guys and something clicked. Seeing him eye to eye, the light-skinned guy looked different. I noticed he had these gorgeous green eyes and a sexy smile. I don't know what changed, but something drew me to him. After conferring with Amy, she agreed he was a good-looking guy.

With the drab way I looked, I definitely wasn't going to say anything to him. Instead I headed back to the bar to seek out more hot water for my third cup of tea. While waiting, I happened to glance back towards my table and saw Amy was no longer there.

I knew she wouldn't just leave my purse unattended, so I looked around and found her at the table where the three guys were seated. She was chatting it up with the green-eyed bald guy. It was just him and her sitting at the table; his friends were nowhere in sight.

Carrying her purse as well as mine, she walked towards me with this huge grin on her face. "I told that guy you thought was cute about you and he wants to talk to you!" I stared at her, confused, and asked her if she had noticed what I currently looked like.

She assured me that he saw me and still wanted to talk to me. I was mortified. It was so high school of her to approach him on my behalf. I wasn't even sure I wanted to talk to him; I simply found him attractive.

Awkwardly, I approached his table carrying my cup of hot water. He introduced himself as Elijah and we shook hands. I wasn't sure if he actually wanted to meet me or if he was just being nice because my friend was so aggressive.

His friends returned from the bathroom as I sat in the 4th chair at their table and apologized if we were interrupting their evening. The other two guys introduced themselves and assured me it was no bother. They told me they were from all over the country and were only in town for a Marines training being held in Virginia.

As Elijah continued to talk, he began to rub me the wrong way. He was very sarcastic, and kind of a smart ass. He didn't know me well enough to poke fun at me, but that didn't stop him. His personality was very strong, and I felt like he was overpowering the group and talking over me.

We exchanged numbers, but I didn't actually plan on contacting him because he had gotten on my nerves in such a short amount of time. He mentioned that their reason for being in came to the city was to party and asked us for suggestions. Amy suggested Adams Morgan because that was her frequent stomping ground. There were a variety of bars to choose from varying in music and the crowds they attracted.

As we all walked out of the restaurant together, Elijah asked what she and I had planned for the rest of the night. In my mind, my plan was to fall asleep, drooling on my pillow because my nose was congested. I couldn't say that out loud, though, so I simply told him we hadn't decided yet.

"Maybe we can hang out later," he suggested. I told him I would talk to Amy and text him to let him know if we were going to go home or go out. We all said goodnight and headed our separate ways.

As Amy and I were walking, we noticed a road blocked off with a glow of bright lights coming from the other end. We thought it was odd and walked to check it out. As we got closer, we saw a few large trucks, a movie crew set up, and a few roaring motorcycles. One bike came flying down the street in our direction then the driver went up on his front tire and came to a stop.

We walked up to the crowd of people that had formed on the sidewalk and one of the bystanders informed us they were filming motorcycle tricks for an upcoming DVD. The bikers would ride up and down the street at full speed, come to a screeching halt in front of a plastic bottle then maneuver their bike on one wheel to come down and crush it with the other wheel. Amy was especially excited to watch their tricks because she'd recently purchased a motorcycle.

As we stood there, I felt my phone vibrating in my back pocket. I looked at it and didn't recognize the number but answered anyway. It was Elijah calling to ask if we had made a decision about what we planned to do next. I told him we hadn't because we were distracted by a movie set.

After determining how far he had parked from where we were, he and his friends walked over to us. The guys feigned interest for a little while then tried to get us to accompany them to Adams Morgan. My cold symptoms were getting worse, which meant I wasn't in the mood to go anywhere but home to rest.

As we all walked back to our prospective vehicles, Amy and I tried to politely deflect their invitations to go out with them. Once I made it to my car, I told everyone goodbye. Elijah walked over to me then asked to see my keychain. As soon as I let go of the keys, he yelled out to his friends that he would be riding with me and they could follow in their truck.

He unlocked my car and got into the driver's seat. After spending several minutes unsuccessfully trying to remove him from the car, I reluctantly got into the passenger side so we could hurry up and get him somewhere and then I would head home.

Once we arrived at the bar, I was going to make up an excuse to leave then bail on them. Amy didn't find either of his friends attractive, but she came along simply because she wanted to make sure I was safe and to execute an exit strategy when needed.

I had to give Elijah turn-by-turn directions since he clearly had no idea where he was going with that being his first time in DC.

During the drive, he ended up ignoring one of the turns and we all ended up driving ten minutes out of the way. As a result of him driving too fast he kept missing opportunities to make a U-turn.

Whenever I'm irritated, I shut down. Instead of snapping at Elijah, I decided to check social media on my phone in silence. I continued to press buttons and open different applications to try and calm myself down. When he sensed I wasn't amused by his antics he finally slowed down enough to get us all back on the right path to our destination.

Amy and his friends who were following us on that wild goose chase didn't find his actions amusing, either. His friends even ended up getting a speeding camera ticket and a red light ticket while following us in the wrong direction. Amy laid into him about how all the unnecessary driving through construction zones was rough on her bike.

Once we made it to the main strip of Adams Morgan, traffic was at a standstill in both directions with no street parking available. Elijah volunteered to pay $20 to park in a garage. I didn't want him to because then I would feel obligated to stay longer, but it was either him pay for a garage or we drive around until all of the bars were closed. Either way, I would have to be there all night, so I sucked it up and agreed to the garage.

His friends walked past the Mad Hatter and told us they wanted to go in, even though Amy advised against it. She knew the music wasn't going to be great but the guys insisted. When we walked in, there were a few people dancing around with no rhythm and the DJ's playlist was playing outdated music.

While inside, we didn't want to crowd the guys, so Amy and I danced near the side of the bar closest to the door in order to make a quick exit. She and I people-watched as I kept one eye on

Elijah and his friends. After a few bad songs that were impossible to dance to, I decided to just sit down at a table. Elijah came over with a round of shots, seemingly trying to repair the impression I had of him from the car ride there.

As soon as he walked away, a girl came up to him and grabbed his hand. I continued to watch the situation unfold to see how he would interact with her. She pulled him close to her and started dancing. She was really putting in work, grinding on him while whipping her hair around. Amy started judging the poor girl's outdated, neon one-piece jumpsuit and the stiff weave she appeared to be wearing. Even with putting forth zero effort and being sick, I looked ten times better than she did.

When the song they were dancing to ended, she said something in his ear then they both headed towards the bar. She proceeded to buy him a drink, which seemed like a waste of money. If Elijah was interested in her then he would've picked up the tab. Although their exchange was amusing, the more I watched, the less confident I was about us speaking after that night.

A few minutes later, he pulled away from the girl and came back over to where I was sitting. After a few shy glances and small talk, he challenged me by saying I looked like I couldn't dance. Obviously that was his way of inviting me to dance with him. I warned him that his new girlfriend, who was eyeballing us from the bar, would get jealous but he told me not to worry about her.

I got out of my seat, turned my back to him, and started dancing against him. I didn't have to do all the dips and hair flips to keep him interested. We danced together for a few songs to the point where my legs were burning. From the corner of my eye, I saw the girl who had brought him a drink accept defeat when he wrapped his arms around me.

I was surprisingly having a good time with him but it was getting late and I was too tired to stay any longer. I told the group I was going to head home. Instead of saying goodnight, Elijah wanted to leave with me. My brain said to politely decline his offer and head to my car by myself but looking into his eyes stopped me from saying no.

Since I lived with my mother at the time, I told him there was no way he could come to my house, so he suggested going back to his hotel. As the night progressed, I had grown to enjoy being with him and I wasn't ready to let him go.

Before we headed out, Amy gave me a talk about being careful and not taking him too seriously. I didn't tell her I was going back to his hotel. Instead, I let her believe I was going home after he walked me to my car. She made me promise to text her once I made it in. I knew if I told her I was going home with Elijah, who I had met merely hours before, she would personally escort me to my car and send him on his way back to his friends.

Just as when we arrived, Elijah and I had to wait in traffic as all of the patrons from the crowded street attempted to exit the crowded area. While sitting in the car, he suddenly leaned over, grabbed my face, and kissed me. Even though he knew I was sick, he still wanted to kiss me. It was endearing that he was seeing me at my worst but was still attracted to me.

As I drove the 30 minute drive to his hotel in Virginia, he sounded like he was feeding me every line in from the book of 'All the Right Things to Say to Get a Woman to Sleep with You'. I didn't want to take anything coming out his mouth seriously. The way the night was going, I figured I would just sleep with him and never speak to him again.

Then he started telling me about how much he enjoyed

being with me and how it had been such a long time since he had felt that way. I drowned out most of it until he said something that struck a cord and changed the way that I felt. I know he was drunk and I should've known it didn't mean anything, but to me, in that moment, it meant something.

I still had the ring my father literally tried to squeeze out of my mom and always wore it on my right ring finger. Elijah took the ring off my right hand and asked me to give him my left hand. Then he placed the ring on my left ring finger and said, "I should just propose to you right now."

Time sort of stopped for a few seconds. Was this what love at first sight looked like? Even though I didn't want to admit it, at some point, when I wasn't looking, I began to fall hard for him.

He continued to tell me how things felt different with me and that one gesture, he had me thinking, maybe he was different. Was it possible that the guy I met and went home with on the first night could turn into something more? A girl could dream.

Finally, we made it to his room and I sent Amy a text saying "I'm in." I did what she asked without telling her exactly where I was 'in' at. Elijah and I started kissing as soon as we got into his hotel room. Then the clothes started to come off. We didn't waste any time.

I could've gone through the charade of saying, "I really just came here to cuddle" or "Maybe we should wait", but we were already in his bed so who was I trying to fool. The only time I felt bad about what we were doing was because I didn't want to pass my cold onto him. Even though I kept bringing it up, he said he didn't care and that I was worth the risk.

We spent that first night together blissfully exploring each other's bodies. Having sex with him was everything I could've wanted and more. I was able to let myself go and just be in the moment. I didn't feel self-conscious about what I looked like and didn't hold back. I just enjoyed how he paid attention to every inch of my body and how beautiful he made me feel.

The next morning, I expected things to be different. I was waiting for him talk about what a busy day he had ahead and rush me out of his room. He never did. Instead, we laid together and talked all morning.

When it was time for me to leave, he initiated the conversation about when he would see me again. I assumed he was being polite, so I told him he was more than welcome to visit my apartment later on in the day. Even if I didn't hear from him again, that night would always be special to me.

On Sundays, it was tradition to watch the local NFL team play with my mom. After stopping to get food, I took a shower and spent the rest of the day lying on the couch, watching football. As the day progressed, what began as a sore throat and the sniffles turned into a full-on raging cold by the time the 4 o'clock game went off.

As the day went on, I was sure I was never going to hear from Elijah again. But that didn't stop me from replaying our night together in my head I couldn't stop smiling.

While day dreaming, I got a text from Elijah requesting my address so he could come over and watch the 8 o'clock football game with me. Within an hour, he was at my door. Since I wasn't feeling well, he told me to lay my head on his lap while we watched TV.

Once the game was over, he got up to leave but before

getting to the door, he asked me to come back to his hotel with him. I had all the reasons in the world to say no: I was sick, I had to work the next morning, and we would have to drive both of our cars for the 45-minute drive back to his hotel. After he pleaded along with his best puppy dog eyes, I quickly packed a small bag, kissed my mom goodbye, and headed to Virginia.

That was how almost every night over the next week went. We spent every night together. I would go home every two days to get more clothes. Every morning I went to work straight from his hotel and went back as soon as I got off.

One night, we agreed to go out and spend time with our friends apart from each other. We had been together so much it was nice to give each other time to miss each other. Around midnight, I got a text from him asking me to meet him at his hotel. Clearly, it worked and he missed me immediately. I told him I would be happy to come, but since he wasn't sure when his friends would be ready to leave, there would be no way for me to get into his room.

After the club, the last thing I wanted to do was hang around a hotel lobby waiting for him to arrive. As soon as I said that, he called the hotel to give them permission to give me a key. I was officially able to come and go as I pleased, even if he wasn't there. It was the out-of-town equivalent of getting a key to a guy's apartment after a week.

I always looked forward to getting off work each day to drive an extra 30 minutes in traffic to his hotel, because it meant I got to spend time with him. Even the smallest moments made me happy. One of my favorites was a random evening when we decided to get something to eat but I didn't have any more casual clothes to wear and I didn't want to wear work clothes for the quick trip out, so I slid on a pair of his jeans. Wearing his pants signified a level of comfort with a guy I had never experienced before. There were no 'boyfriend jeans' in the world that could compare to what it felt like to wear his clothes.

Our relationship moved pretty fast. The following Sunday, he and one of the guys from the first night we met all drove to my grandparents' house for Sunday dinner. While Elijah and his friend sat in the living room, my grandmother said to me, "After watching you all together, I think they both like you." I couldn't tell his friend liked me but when I looked at the two of them, I could only see Elijah.

We had created our own world together, mainly consisting of being in his hotel room. I allow myself to think about what would happen after he left Virginia; I just tried to enjoy the time we had together. I took every opportunity I had to be with him so if my friends wanted to see me, oftentimes they came to visit me at his hotel.

Part of his training was practicing a special form of physical combat used by the Marines. The training was extremely physically demanding, and that was his excuse for always wanting to stay in. One day in particular, the training was so vigorous he was overcome with full body cramps.

As soon as he called and told me, I went into full caretaker mode. Before arriving, I stopped at a convenience store and picked up a bunch of snacks he liked and plenty of fluids for him to drink. After letting myself in, he stayed on the bed, only moving gingerly when necessary. He had ice packs strategically placed all over his body and looked miserable.

Amy came out to Virginia after work with me to hang out since I had become so absorbed in being with Elijah. She and I ordered pizza while we laughed and caught up as he laid on the bed in pain, observing us. We poked fun at him a few times but mainly talked as if he wasn't here. Whatever we talked about I didn't mind saying in front of him. I felt like we had known each other much longer than a week and a half.

There was only one person in my life who wasn't a fan of his and that was Jade. She lived not too far from where he was staying. She called me one afternoon to meet for some girl time since she needed to vent about boy trouble. I invited her over to talk, and we ended up going out for lunch with Elijah and another one of his training buddies.

She and I were just being our normal outgoing selves. I would say hi to the bus boys as they walked by and we would joke around with the server. Elijah thought we were being condescending, even though our intentions were just to be nice. He kept chastising us like we were his children if we said or did anything he didn't like. By the end of lunch, there was an awkward silence at the table. I could tell that if Elijah said another word, Jade would've bitten his head off.

He had been extremely outspoken and opinionated from the moment I met him. He would never hesitate to say exactly what was on his mind. He was also very sarcastic and if you weren't familiar with him, it could be interpreted as rude or mean-spirited. He and Amy got along well because they had similar personalities, going back and forth with jabs. Jade was much more sensitive, like me, so he rubbed her the wrong way.

She and I thought a lot alike because we had a lot of the same experiences with the opposite sex. Our negative experiences allowed us to connect and understand each other. He misinterpreted her venting as man-bashing.

As discussed how he disliked her views on men, I tried to explain to him that she had been my friend long before I met him.

He didn't have to like all of my friends, but he did have to be respectful. During my next lunch date with Jade, I made the mistake of mentioning something Elijah said about her. For the remainder of his time in town, she chose not to see me if it meant she had to interact with him.

For their last night in town, the Marines staying in the hotel decided to have a farewell party in their lobby and outdoor patio area. They had pizza, beer, and liquor for everyone to enjoy. I had to go home prior to heading to his hotel and by the time I had gotten there, all of the pizza was gone and everyone was drunk.

I spotted Elijah joking with a group of guys outside on the patio, being the life of the party. Before I walked over to him, I could tell by watching his interactions that most of the guys there admired and respected him, which I found attractive. After mingling with some of the wives and girlfriends, I was ready to retire upstairs. It was his last night in town, and I wanted to spend some time alone with him before going to sleep.

Once we got upstairs, I went to lie down, thinking he was right behind me. Instead, he told me he wanted to go back downstairs to continue drinking. I snapped at him that if he wanted to spend the whole night getting drunk with his buddies he could've told me that before I drove all the way out there.

My feelings were hurt because it didn't seem like he cared whether I was there or not. I told him I was just going to go back home and let him enjoy his night of partying. My blow-up may have been uncalled for, but I was dreading saying goodbye to him and that wasn't the way I saw our last night together going. Even though I was exhausted, I drove all the way out there thinking he wanted to spend quality time with me.

He slowly backed me up against the wall and told me to

calm down. He didn't want me to leave, and he assured me he wanted us to be together that night. He went on to say how he had grown to care about me more than he expected to. He had never really talked to me about what would happen when he left but during his drunken proclamation, he made me feel like we would be in each other's lives no matter the distance between us. He never did go back downstairs.

The next morning, I had planned on heading to work after seeing him off to the base where they were holding an award ceremony for the Marines who participated in the training course. Since he always left before me, I usually laid in bed and watched him get ready. That morning, I made sure to get out of bed and hug him a little longer.

I took my time before leaving the room, trying to hold on to the memories created there. I stopped in the lobby where they served complimentary breakfast every morning to pick up a coffee and bagel before heading to my car. One of the wives I had met the night before was in the lobby with her kids.

She recognized me and asked if I was going to the award ceremony. I told her I wasn't going to be able to make it because I had to work. I mentioned, even if I did want to go, I didn't know how to get there. She insisted I follow her and some of the other wives in my car so I could attend the ceremony. "Is there any way you could make it? I'm sure he would want you to be there."

I really did want to see him graduate and since I was the only person outside of the military he knew there, maybe he would appreciate my support. I called my job and told them I was having car trouble so I would be late. Elijah had a flight to catch that afternoon, so I would make my way to work afterwards.

The sleeveless shirt and open-toed shoes I had on wouldn't fly on the military base. While the wives were getting ready, I drove over to the nearest Target and picked up a modest red, three-quarter-sleeve shirt and some ballet flats. When I returned to the hotel, everyone was gathering in the lobby to help each other load their kids into the car.

Upon entering the base, there were soldiers directing guests on where to park. I parked first but waited for the ladies I followed there to unload their kids because I didn't want to walk in by myself. As soon as I walked into the auditorium I spotted Elijah talking with a group of guys in the front of the room by the stage.

I was extremely hesitant to go over and let him know I was there since he didn't invite me, nor did I tell him I was coming. As I approached him, I kept hoping he wasn't disappointed or creeped out. It would've been embarrassing if he told me to leave because sound traveled far throughout the small auditorium. Everyone in the room would think I was some sort of stalker.

When he finally looked over and saw me, he sort of froze with a look of confusion on his face. Luckily, a smile replaced his initial shock shortly after, and he reached out to give me a hug. He was definitely surprised that I was there but happy I cared enough to skip work in order to support him.

When the ceremony started, I was beaming like the proud girlfriend I wished I was. I took pictures, I applauded every little thing, and I cheered whenever Elijah received an award. He worked very hard to receive the highest cumulative score in his class.

He did receive an award for outstanding performance and while I was proud of him, I was disappointed he didn't win the congeniality award. Different things are important to different people, and competing to show he was the best was important to him, not building friendships.

After we headed back to his hotel, I sat with him while he packed the rest of his belongings for the flight back home to California. He mentioned that he had planned to go home for a few days, and then his mother was flying to him so they could take a road trip to his hometown of Milwaukee together. Although he would be busy, he assured me that we would keep in touch after he got back.

We hugged one last time as we stood outside next to our cars. He walked away, paused before he got into the car, looked back at me and said, "I really thought you would cry when I left." I laughed because I thought I would, too.

CHAPTER 9

2009 II

After Elijah returned to California, I did my best not to constantly check my phone for missed calls or texts because I knew he was busy getting things in order for his mother's arrival. A week had gone by and I still hadn't heard from him. My patience was beginning to wear thin waiting to hear from him. I went from seeing him almost every day for two weeks to dead silence.

My mind ran rampant with different scenarios. Maybe he had a girlfriend or a wife back home that he kept from me. It was possible he dropped his phone in the toilet and didn't back up his contacts. Worst of all, maybe he was just using me for sex while he was in town.

Instead of continuing to drive myself crazy, I bit the bullet and called him. The phone rang for a while and I thought he was probably looking at my name on his screen and purposefully not picking up. After what seemed like several minutes, he picked up and said, "Hey, lady." Finally, I could breathe a sigh of relief that at least he wasn't ignoring me.

I didn't want to immediately bombard him with questions about why I hadn't heard from him, so I started with small talk. We talked about how being back home was going and what he was doing to prepare for his road trip. He was currently getting his car checked out in preparation for the long ride to Wisconsin with his mom.

After just a few minutes, the feelings that were wavering before that phone call came flooding back. As we were getting off the phone, he said he would call me soon. My expectations were low based on past experience, but I tried not to let my skepticism show.

To my surprise, later on that night, I received a phone call from him. His mom was taking a nap while they rode through some dark and deserted area, so he called me to help keep him awake. We stayed on the phone for hours, mainly talking about his family and how he felt like he was the glue keeping them all together. I wanted to mention the possibility of coming to visit him, but it didn't seem like the right time.

While he was in Milwaukee, the phone calls and texts became scarce. I could feel him slipping away again, and I was desperate to get back to what we had in Virginia. I did my best to give him his space, knowing he was seeing many family members and friends he hadn't seen in a while. I decided to call him one Sunday after leaving my grandparents' house.

He was at a gathering at his mom's house but he stepped out of the room to take my call. I didn't want to interrupt his quality time, but he insisted he wanted to talk to me at least for a few minutes. With it constantly being on my mind, bubbling up in my throat every time I talked to him, I threw out the idea of me coming to visit him, hoping he wouldn't cringe or laugh.

He paused for a few seconds then said, "Yeah, that sounds like a plan." As soon as he agreed, I was planning the entire trip in my head. We picked a weekend that worked for both of us, and I told him

I would let him know once I had made all of my arrangements.

As my visit approached, he and I spoke almost every day. A few nights before my departure, we discussed what we could do while I was there. One thing he stated was definitely not on the agenda was me meeting his mother. His reasoning was that he didn't want to introduce her to any females unless he was sure they would be around for a long time.

That statement really stung—not because I was looking forward to meeting his mother but because he still wasn't sure if he wanted me in his life. If he didn't see me in his future, what was the point of me visiting? His messages were conflicting, and I began to feel like he was leading me on. I decided to get off the phone before my emotions caused me to say something I'd regret.

I tried not to let his words affect me too much. I had to respect the fact that not everyone was as open with introducing people to their family as I was. If I continued to overanalyze and dissect the meaning of every word he said, I wasn't going to enjoy my trip.

The time came for me to board my plane and head to Milwaukee. My flight landed early in the morning and Elijah was supposed to pick me up from the airport. I texted him to let him know I was taking off and once I landed, I called him to let him know I arrived, but he didn't answer. I called again, but he didn't pick up.

The annoyance began to set in. I felt forgotten about and abandoned. After 30 minutes, my phone finally rang. He told me he had overslept but was coming right away. Being stuck at the airport in a city I've never been to wasn't my ideal way of starting my trip.

When he finally arrived, my greeting was pretty dry. We

drove in silence for a few minutes until he announced we were
going to take a detour on the way to my hotel. He showed me all of
the schools he attended as a child and a few neighborhoods he used
to live in. I thought it was sweet that he wanted me to see where he
grew up and by the end of the tour, my mood had improved
significantly.

Then we stopped in front of a cute one-level house with a
fenced in front yard. I asked him whose house it was, and he said it
was his mother's house. I was shocked because less than a week ago,
he told me there was no way I was going to meet his mother. I asked
him what changed and he simply stated, "It felt like the right thing to
do."

In an instant, I became overwhelmed with anxiety and
excitement. I hadn't mentally prepared myself to meet his mother, so
I only had a few seconds from the car to the house to gather myself.
Prior to facing an uncomfortable or serious situation, ideally I
would've had time to mentally prepare.

I had never met the mother of anyone I wanted to date
seriously, so I wasn't sure how to approach the situation. Did I want
to come off as sweet and innocent, or was I going to take the funny
and outspoken approach? Was the outfit I had on appropriate?
How much information did I want to divulge? I definitely would
leave out how I slept with her son the first night I met him.

Once we got inside, he told me his mother was at work but
she would be home in about an hour. The house was very
personalized and welcoming; it was easy to feel comfortable there.
Since I had time before she arrived, I began to observe all the photos
and collectibles around the home and realized there was a Native
American theme.

I asked Elijah what the significance of those items were

and he told me he was half-Black and half-Native American. He was surprised I couldn't tell. Given the diversity of each ethnicity, I had given up on trying to figure it out myself long ago. People constantly assumed I was either mixed or from some island. Granted, any of these things could've been true about my ancestors, but I simply considered myself Black.

Before long, I heard keys rattling in the front door. His mother walked into the house and the room seemed to close in on me a little bit. When we were introduced, I could definitely tell she was Native American. She had this beautiful long, brown hair that was braided down her back. I could see where Elijah got his looks from; minus the hair, they had the same facial features and beautiful hazel-green eyes.

They started bantering back and forth after he introduced us, that was when I realized they also shared the same personality. She was a very outgoing and sharp woman, always ready with a response when Elijah said something sarcastic. They seemed to have a fun and open relationship that reminded me of how my mom and I were with each other.

When I'm in a new surrounding or around people I'm not familiar with, I tend to be very quiet. I'd rather observe in silence, especially when the other people in the room know each other already. As they continued to talk, his mother looked at me and asked, "Are you just going to sit there and look pretty or are you going to speak up?" At that point, I needed to get comfortable, and quickly.

I wasn't sure what to talk about, so I brought up the fact that I attended Elijah's award ceremony. I could tell he was her pride and joy, mainly because she kept joking that he was her favorite son. Her eyes lit up as we both talked about how hard he worked while in training. Slowly, I started to feel like we were all bonding.

The unexpected introduction to his mother was one of the more enjoyable moments from my trip to Milwaukee. Our conversation flowed and at times, she and I spoke as if Elijah wasn't in the room. Later on that night, we all went out to dinner. The entire time I was sitting there, I hoped for more evenings together like that.

On the way home, we stopped at the grocery store to pick up drinks for the hotel room. I grabbed a bottle of vodka while Elijah retrieved mixers. As his mom watched from afar, I caught her gazing at us with a smirk on her face as we interacted. I could tell by talking to her that she was a good judge of character and very straightforward, so if I could get a seal of approval from her that could only mean good things for our future.

After dropping his mother off, we headed back to my hotel. Elijah got ice from the machine in the hallway and then we settled into bed with a couple of drinks. After having such an unexpected experience, we didn't say much. He just pulled me into him and gave the kind of passionate kiss that always made me melt.

For the trip, I packed some candles and lingerie to show him to try and spice things up. I didn't have much experience in seduction but I hoped he would appreciate my efforts. That night seemed like the perfect night to pull out all the stops. While I set everything up, I made him go into the bathroom and promise not to come out until I called him.

I quickly changed into a black one-piece, set the tea light candles around the room, and lit them. As I was lighting the last candle, I could see him peeking around the corner. Even though he didn't listen, I stood up and showed him what I had on. He silently walked over to me with a huge grin on his face. I was just as smitten with him as I was after our first night together.

I missed the feeling of having his arms wrapped around my waist. I missed running my finger over his lips before I kissed him. I missed the way he made me feel like he couldn't wait to have me. The outfit I put on quickly came off as he picked me up and laid me down on the bed. The candles melted away as we got lost in each other.

The alcohol was running through my body, thoughts of how much I had missed him were running through my head, while his hands were running all over my body. We held onto each other like we were connected.

His sweat was dripping all over my body as I focused on nothing but enjoying the way he felt inside of me. Suddenly he stopped moving, I assumed to keep himself from coming and make the sex last longer. When he didn't resume, I asked him if everything was okay. As he rubbed his face against mine, he moaned into my ear that he just came.

Over the course of our time together in Virginia, we had stopped using condoms so since I wasn't on birth control, he would pull out before ejaculating. I laid there panting for a few seconds until it dawned on me that he was still inside of me. Panic began to set in. I asked him why he didn't pull out and he just sort of peered at me with a blank look on his face.

While intoxicated, I don't believe he really concerned himself with the possible result of coming inside of me. While I was fussing at him about what he did, he simply poured himself another drink. Seemingly not paying me any attention, his phone began to ring. I told him he better not answer it while we were both naked, but he continued to ignore me.

He sat down next to me, speaking to the person on the other end as if he had just woke up or something. When he got off the phone, he told me it was his cousin calling to ask him to pick her up. She had gone out to a party and the people she came with weren't ready to leave, but she was. I agreed to shelve our conversation, threw on some sweats, and got in the passenger seat of his car to go get her.

Once we arrived at the house, his cousin was already standing outside on the sidewalk. She got into the back seat and the two of them immediately started talking without any introduction. I felt invisible as they continued to talk to each other like I wasn't sitting there. She went on and on about her boy troubles, how she hated her job, and caught him up on the rest of what was happening in her life. The entire car ride they didn't acknowledge me once.

When she finally got out of the car, I had yet another reason to lay into him. It seemed like throughout the trip, there were a lot of little things he did that would get under my skin. The little things were the most significant to me, and I noticed everything. Not introducing me to friends or family when we were together and answering the phone in the middle of a post-sex discussion bothered me.

We got back to the hotel after a silent car ride and resumed our earlier conversation. We both agreed I should take a Plan B pill the next day, and then we went to sleep on opposite sides of the bed. I tried not to let every little thing ruin my mood, but his actions were creating friction during my trip.

The next day ended up being a culmination of all of the things that had gone wrong before. The beginning of the day went well. On the way back to his mom's house, we picked up lunch at their favorite sub shop. Then we made plans to go to the movies later on that evening. I looked up movie times while he changed his clothes, and we headed to the theater.

The ride to the movie theater was strangely quiet. Every so often, I would glance over at him but he seemed to be content sitting in silence, so I didn't say anything. As we pulled into the parking lot of the outdoor shopping center, we passed by the entrance of the movie theater. I also noticed we were passing multiple open parking spaces and getting further away from the theater.

As we passed what seemed like the tenth open parking space, I was so annoyed that I snapped at him about why we were driving so far away from the theater. Dryly, he replied that he didn't want to worry about getting a ticket, so he wanted to park in the lot at the other end of the shopping center. If change for the meter was what he needed, I could have provided that.

It was a cold fall night in Milwaukee and the energy between us was equally as frigid by the time he parked. Now I had to walk unnecesarily far in 30 degree weather to get to our destination, and I was less than pleased. When I got out of the car, there was a little extra pep in my step so I could get to the movie theater faster, not only to escape the weather but also to make our movie time.

Apparently, I was walking too fast because every time I looked back, Elijah was further and further behind me. I went to cross the street and he was so far behind, I went ahead and crossed to wait for him inside. There were still no words exchanged between us as we walked up the stairs to buy tickets for the movie we agreed upon.

After we announced our selection, the woman behind the ticket counter informed us that the movie we chose was sold out. I asked him if he wanted to wait for the next movie, to which he replied no. There we were once again, walking silently back to his car.

On our way back to the car, I decided to walk behind him to observe his body language. From what I could see, he wasn't happy. Inside the car, I asked him what was wrong and he quipped, "Nothing." Obviously *something* was wrong because he had a look of irritation on his face and he wouldn't look at me. So I asked him again, hoping his answer would change. It didn't.

I tried to move past the tension in the car, so I asked if there was something else he wanted to do instead of the movie. He snapped a quick, "No", so I stopped trying. We spent the rest of the ride back to my hotel in silence.

Once we got into the room, I had endured his silent treatment long enough. What did he even have to be mad about? If he wasn't going to talk then why come all the way up to my room just to ignore me?

Not only was he mute but he did everything he could to physically distance himself from me. While I was seated on the bed, he sat across the room at the desk, clicking away on his phone. After a ten-minute standoff, I asked him if he was going to act that way the rest of the night. Without even looking up from his phone, he replied, "Act what way?"

When I asked him why he was sitting across the room by himself, not speaking, he told me he was trying to book a flight for his friend. I told him he didn't have to do that from across the room in silence. I asked him if I had said or done something to make him upset and he continued to say nothing, eyes glued to his phone.

My patience with him was wearing thin. Since he seemingly didn't want to tell me what was wrong, I just kept repeating myself until he gave me something more than 'nothing'.

When that didn't work, I just poured out everything that was weighing on me.

I told him that he was being rude, unappreciative, and was behaving like a child. I'm sure most of the things I said were out of line, but I saw green and couldn't take my foot off the gas. I felt so frustrated and unappreciated. I had paid for a flight and hotel to spend time with him and in return, he spent most of the time treating me like I didn't exist or that my feelings didn't matter.

Finally, tired of me badgering him, he divulged why he had been acting that way all night. He was upset with me that I walked ahead of him on the way to the movie theater. That was worth ruining an entire evening during the short time we had together.

To him, it was a sign of disrespect. As all of the other couples were walking side by side or hand in hand, but we didn't even look like we knew each other. Coming from someone who gets upset about the smallest and sometimes pettiest things, I didn't see the situation as seriously as he did. My intention was never to disrespect him. I explained to him that my actions were a result of trying to rush out of the cold weather.

Even with an apology and explanation, he didn't let up. I wasn't going to sit there all night begging for his forgiveness for walking briskly because he decided to park half a mile away from our destination. He continued to play on his phone and made no effort to pay me any attention so I just went to sleep.

I woke up to a dark and quiet room at 4 o'clock in the morning. I felt next to me and the bed was empty. My mind began to race as I turned on the lights. No sign of Elijah. He wasn't in the bed, not on the couch, and not in the chair.

Did he really leave in the middle of the night without saying anything? I was cursing him out intensely in my head as I got out of bed to go to the bathroom. When I looked down, there he was, lying on the floor next to the coffee table with no blanket, just a small pillow from the couch under his head.

Any anger I had melted away. It broke my heart that he felt like he had to sleep on the floor instead of getting in the bed. Especially a hotel room floor—who knows what goes on in those rooms. I woke him up and coaxed him into bed. Groggily, he got up and laid down next to me. I turned the lights back off and tried to go back to sleep.

Moments later, he turned over and wrapped his arms around me. He whispered in my ear, "I don't want to fight anymore. I miss you." Even though we had been with each other the entire night, I missed him, too. I went to bed feeling like if we could get through that trip, then maybe we did stand a chance.

Elijah was never able to come back to Maryland to visit me since he had a strict military schedule. I was still trying to keep hope alive for our relationship so a month after I got back from Wisconsin, I went to visit him in California. That time, it would just be me and him.

It was in my nature to try and do unexpected, personalized things for the people I cared about. Before I headed to California, I drew a picture of him from the day of his awards ceremony. Drawing and painting were something I had been doing since high school, so I drew here and there to hone my skills. I was so excited to show him the end result that I presented it to him as soon as I got in his car at the airport.

He held the drawing in his hands and praised me on how

well I did. Then he sort of threw it in the backseat of his car. I put so much effort into drawing that picture. I went over it multiple times, erasing and redrawing certain features to make sure it look as close as possible to the original picture.

When he tossed it in the back of his car, he treated it like it was discarded takeout trash. I looked back and could already see wrinkles in the paper. That bothered me so much, but I kept it hidden in order to not start off another trip on a sour note.

As we were driving, I began to recognize some of the exits from the highway. I got the sense that we weren't far from my cousin's house. I hadn't been there in years, but I distinctly remembered the scenery. I asked if he would mind me calling my family to see how far they were from the exit we were on. I could tell he didn't want to say yes, but he agreed.

I got ahold of my second cousin and it turned out they were less than ten minutes away. They gave me their address and we headed to their house. I didn't want to stay long because I could tell Elijah was getting fidgety, so our visit lasted less than 30 minutes.

I hugged everyone and told them we might be back in the next day or so. They made me promise I would see them again before I went back home. By the look on Elijah's face, I could tell that wasn't going to happen.

We pulled up to his house and it looked like an adult lived there, not the bachelor pad I was expecting. There was no grass because it was the desert but other than that, it was an adorable one-level stone house with a garage and a fence. It wasn't military housing; he was renting directly from the owner.

There wasn't much to show me on the inside, but he gave me a tour anyway. The refrigerator was pretty bare and the living room was set up with every game console known to man. He also collected classic Disney movies, which I found endearing. His room had a bed and a dresser with not much else. It didn't look truly lived in. Decorating or hanging pictures wasn't high on his list of things to do.

He had to work the first day I was there, so I planned to surprise him with a home-cooked meal when he got home. I called my grandmother to ask her for some recipes so I could make something based on the few items he had in his kitchen. I even walked to the CVS about a mile down the road to get a few things he liked to drink and snack on.

I set up the small table in the kitchen with place settings as I cooked fried chicken, broccoli, rice, and biscuits. I was sure that when he saw all I had done, he would be blown away by efforts. Instead, the only thing he could focus on was me walking all the way to the store by myself. "If something happened to you while you were out, it would be my responsibility because you're my guest."

As an adult, walking to a store in broad daylight a mile away didn't seem like a major security issue. His ranting about me leaving the house ruined the excitement I had about the dinner I prepared. To get him to stop talking about it, I agreed not to walk anywhere else without running it past him first.

The rest of the trip was relatively uneventful. He didn't really plan anything for us to do. We hung out with a few of his friends, went out to eat once or twice, and had a lot of great sex. He had to work most of the days I was there so it gave me a glimpse into what being his significant other felt like.

We talked about where we saw ourselves in the next few years. He wanted to get out of the Marines and start working as a contractor overseas. The significant increase in salary and decrease of stress as a civilian working with the military was driving his decision-making.

Apparently, he was going to make his choice in the next few weeks. If he did choose to be a contractor, he would leave and begin working in Afghanistan indefinitely within the next few months. I was hoping I was going to be a part of his future, but with him moving to another continent, it didn't look promising.

On the way back to the airport, I wasn't as hopeful for our future as I was on the way there but I appreciated the time we were able to spend together. When things were good, they were great, but it just seemed like during that time in our lives, what he had wasn't strong enough to develop into anything more. If he was going to leave and work halfway across the world, he wasn't prepared to make a relationship work.

When we said goodbye, I could tell it was going to be the last hug I would get from him in a long time. We didn't even kiss. I didn't go home feeling hopeful. I didn't go home wondering when I would see him again. I was ready to let him go.

I thought our story was going to be a love story that withstood the test of time and distance, but life got in the way. No matter how much I tried, his mind and his heart were not going to belong to me. Elijah and I weren't the meet, fall in love, and live happily ever after fairytale I had hoped for. It felt like a period had been written at the end of the last sentence of our short love story.

CHAPTER 10

2010

The only thing in my life that was going to be constant was work, so I threw myself into that. While I received promotions in my title, my checks still remained the same. Amy had recently started a new position as a Training Technician for an independent company. One of her coworkers was leaving, so she did everything she could to get me a job with her.

I was comfortable at my job, but there was no more room for advancement. At the most, my salary was going to increase to $37,000 a year, which wasn't much if I wanted to live on my own. As nervous as I was about leaving after 3 years, it was time for a change. Not only did I have the opportunity to make over $75,000 a year, but working with a friend would make the transition easier. I never imagined I could make that much money without a Master's degree.

After Amy put in a good word for me to her bosses, I interviewed for the job that same week. I thought the interview went really well, but I received no follow-up phone call about the position over the next week. We weren't sure what to think. When she tried to inquire about the status of my application, she only received a generic response about them still processing applicants.

Finally, I received a phone call from a Human Resources representative two weeks later that I had gotten the position. I was sad to leave my current job because everyone was so kind-hearted and they appreciated my hard work. Unfortunately, appreciation wasn't going to pay the bills, so I had to seize the opportunity to more than double my salary.

The work environment at my new job started off great. I was working in the Asset Forfeiture Division at the headquarters of one of the oldest federal law enforcement agencies alongside those highest in the agency. Almost every day, I would see the Director in the lunch room, and I had an email directory of almost everyone who worked for every government agency.

Having a job with so much responsibility while still being able to travel across the country to assist with the setup of conferences seemed too good to be true. The job was exactly what I went to school for, and it was rewarding to feel like I was putting my education to use. Not to mention I felt very established when I told people where I worked.

My job was to assist with every aspect of training field agents handling asset forfeitures in the field. I would order and ship materials across the country, create training schedules, coordinate with the head of each field office as well as develop documents and presentations for trainings. There were three training technicians altogether, so we split up the field offices equally.

As soon as I started to settle in, Amy began to go through tumultuous times with one of our government managers. We not only had contract supervisors to answer to but also government employees. Twice the managers meant twice the people scrutinizing you.

One of the government managers who had previously

raved about Amy's work ethic had flipped the switch on her. Suddenly, nothing she did was right, her workload was gradually decreasing, and she was being embarrassed in front of the staff by managers as they pointed out even the smallest mistakes she made in every meeting.

During one of our trainings at the headquarters, she came to me and said, "They're going to fire me." At first, I thought she was being paranoid until she detailed all of the things that had been happening. From then on, she had to triple-check her work before turning it in and do everything she could to fly under the radar.

She and I had different start times, so I left earlier than she did. On my way home from work, she called me. We often called each other for assistance with work, so I answered expecting to help her with the training she was running. Instead, she told me that after she had worked a full day and stayed late to complete some of her assignments, management called her into the office and let her go.

I couldn't believe how quickly things went south for her, seemingly for no reason. When she asked why she was being fired, they couldn't give her any legitimate reasons except for her not completing assignments to their standards. She was leaving the office as she was talking to me with all of the items from her desk in a box.

I asked how she was feeling and she said relieved. She had been so stressed out the past few weeks. Since she had seen it coming, she no longer had anxiety about her fate and didn't have to deal with the unrealistic expectations from people at work who were never going to be happy no matter how well she did. She told me what traps they set for her in the hopes that I wouldn't find myself in the same predicament. She warned me to watch my back and to not trust anyone. Even though I always made sure to get my work done prior to its due date and triple checked my assignments before turning them in, I heeded her advice.

After Amy left, work was lonely. Eventually, someone from within the office was promoted to fill her position. Amelia was a quiet and polite Middle Eastern girl. She had been with the agency for a while but seemed to have trouble fitting in and getting her work done on time. Regardless of her perceived shortcomings the managers loved her for some reason. To them, she could do no wrong.

Since she had worked previously in the data entry department, they tasked her with creating presentations based on her knowledge of that subject. When I had to create certain presentations, the managers recommended that I consult with her. Many times, she would provide me with presentations she previously used and I would tailor them to my needs.

As time went on, we had a series of management changes. Around the same time, our contract manager was fired and our government manager was replaced. The higher-ups made a lot of changes because they felt like our division wasn't performing to the best of its abilities.

The new government manager was a Black female in her late thirties. She had a young son she would bring to work on a weekly basis to cover for gaps in child care. I didn't see anyone else bringing their kids to work, but I assumed she had some sort of leniency because he was there at least once a week. As soon as she started, she stressed how she was there to support us and that her door was always open.

I never sought her out for help, but she took a particular interest in constantly commenting on my clothing choices or the way I did my job. Never before were my clothes a problem, but to her, they were too form-fitting and she told me I needed to "think about how my outfits made other people in the office feel."

I was in my early twenties with hips, a decent-sized ass, and a small waist with long legs. Certain clothes on me were going to show off my curves even if I wasn't trying. No matter what I wore, it was a problem to her. I wanted to look professional, but at the same time I didn't see anything wrong with wearing clothes that accentuated my shape.

By no means was I coming into the office looking like I was headed to the club, but I wasn't going to start wearing potato sacks to please her. Other women would continue to come in with skin-tight pants or extremely short skirts. But every time my manager saw me, she would ask me to put a sweater on over whatever I was wearing. Every single day, she had a criticism or comment about my appearance or my work.

Within a matter of weeks, I had gone from having my dream job to being in a living nightmare. Every day I began to dread going to work. When I was off, I would sit at home, stressed out about dealing with another day of feeling bullied about what I looked like. It seemed like I was unfairly being singled out. No matter what changes I made, the hits kept on coming.

One afternoon, I was called into a meeting where both the government and contract managers were present. Apparently, they had been discussing how poorly I was doing for a long time and they claimed they had received multiple complaints about me from the field staff. I was completely blindsided. Since the field staff communicated directly with me, there wasn't a single person I could think of who would have complained.

As soon as I left the meeting, I confided with a fellow training technician I had become close with, Billy, about the managers' comments. He agreed that their allegations were baseless and they seemed personal. He suggested I reach out to the field staff so I could address any possible issues I may not have been aware of.

When I got back to my desk, I compiled the list of field agents I had worked with recently. There were a handful of people I had a great rapport with, so I emailed them asking them to share any concerns or feedback about their experience with me. Every single person responded with nothing but positive accolades.

Every single one of them also agreed to write an email to my managers letting them know how pleased they were with my contributions. I compiled all of those emails, my previous positive evaluations, and my history of timeliness turning in my assignments then put them in a folder next to my desk. Whenever I was summoned to a meeting, I would bring that folder just in case it was an ambush.

I tried to put all of the personal attacks out of my mind and find ways to boost my spirits. Sitting at a desk for 8 hours combined with stress eating at the buffet around the corner from work almost every day caused me to gain a few pounds. Since looking your best generally helped you feel your best, I started making healthier food and beverage choices, drinking more water, and preparing my own meals to bring to work.

As more opportunities became available to travel and gain more knowledge, including being a presenter at conferences, I would jump at them. Getting out of the office any chance I could was what kept me holding on. Not to mention that being a presenter was going to look great on my résumé. I also signed up for outside training courses to show I was taking an initiative to develop my skills, making me a more valuable and versatile employee.

A conference in Philadelphia was coming up and I was

tasked to be a presenter. The date of my departure was quickly approaching, so I worked on the materials I was going to use with Amelia. I sat with her over several days and took most of her advice on the edits needed to finalize my PowerPoint presentation.

When it came time for the training technicians to go over their work for upcoming events with the managers, I shared with them what I was going to present in Philadelphia. Once I was finished, the room fell quiet and the meeting turned into a bashing session. Everything about the presentation I showed them was wrong. They responded as if I had given them nothing but gibberish.

I felt like the reaction I received was undeserved. I explained that I had gone with their advice from previous meetings and worked off a presentation Amelia had recently used. If it was good enough for her, why was it a pile of garbage coming from me?

There was no response about the double standard, just more criticism of my work. Finally, one of the contract managers said, "After viewing what you have so far, we think it's best if you don't go to Philadelphia at all." In that moment, I knew exactly how Amy felt before she got fired. No one could keep me from believing that the managers were doing anything they could to get rid of me.

My entire body was on fire and my face was flushed. I knew it was time to do something to protect myself from being canned. I left the meeting and immediately called my human resources representative, Julie. Billy joined me in a meeting room with her on speaker phone as I told her everything that transpired over the last few weeks. She was stunned.

She told me to stay in the meeting room and that she was going to contact my managers to see what the real issue was. Sitting in that room felt like I was in the waiting room at a hospital, waiting for my test results to come back. Over the last few months, my stress level had reached an all-time high and my self-esteem an all-time low. I couldn't sleep and I couldn't figure out how to keep my mind off of my work conditions. Most of my evenings were spent at home, brought to tears thinking about what I might face at work the next day.

Julie called me back after only a few minutes and told me my government managers expressed that they wanted me off the contract. Their response wasn't surprising, but it was upsetting nonetheless. When she asked for the cause of them wanting to get rid of me, they couldn't give her a specific reason.

She told me, "The best thing for you to do is quit. It's better to leave on your own terms before the situation gets worse." Since I was 16 years old, I had always been employed. I never quit a job unless it was to start another one. If I abruptly quit that job, I had no other source of income to rely on.

Fear overcame me because I had an apartment, car, and various other bills that I was responsible for. How was I going to pay them without a job? Then I had to remind myself that no amount of money was worth sacrificing my mental health. Getting back my peace of mind was more important than trying to stick it out at a job where my managers did everything they could to mentally break me down. Not to mention if I didn't leave on my own terms, it wouldn't be long before they found a reason to fire me.

Billy sat next to me in silence while all of those thoughts ran through my head. It didn't take long for me to decide what my next course of action would be. I was going to head to my office, pack up my things, and immediately notify management that I was quitting. Providing two weeks' notice would've been preferable but after the way I had been treated, I didn't feel like I owed them the courtesy.

As I walked two separate resignation letters to my government manager and then to my contract managers' desk, the cloud of darkness that had been hovering over me began to move away. My mind felt so much clearer, the sun shined brighter through the windows, and I was able to finally breathe.

My desk was nearly boxed up when my contract manager came to my office and did her best to feign surprise that I was leaving. There was no longer a need for me to play nice, so I responded with one-word answers and went back to packing. She continued to ask about what my plans were after I left and what the particular reason was for my sudden departure. I could tell she wasn't concerned about my well-being and was just being nosey, so I stopped responding altogether. After a few seconds of awkward silence, she informed me she would have to escort me out of the building and that she needed to confiscate my government ID. I simply responded, "Okay."

On the way out of the building, my head was held high as I passed the rows of offices leading to the elevator. Some people were surprised to see me leaving, but a few people knew what I had been going through and were happy to finally see me free. Eventually, everyone would find out through office gossip why I had left so abruptly.

Having a job where I earned a great salary and was able to travel all over the country was a blessing. However, having a stress free, positive, and hopeful state of mind was priceless. As I walked to my car, I assured myself that things could only go up from there. I also promised myself that I would never compromise my sanity for a paycheck ever again.

CHAPTER 11

2011

Before leaving the ATF, I had dreams of opening an organic restaurant in DC. Not only did I want to serve food from local organic farms, but I also wanted to provide local artists a place to perform and even sell their artwork. My goal was to mesh a New York-style venue with organic food that didn't compromise taste.

If I was able to rent enough space, there could be a stage for local bands to play on certain nights, then open mic nights or karaoke on others. The vibe was going to be casual and inclusive. It wouldn't matter what you looked like, where you were from, or what you liked to listen to; I wanted everyone to feel welcome. I had already started a business plan, written a menu, and researched local organic food and furniture vendors.

Since I didn't have a job lined up, I thought it would be best to start looking at hospitality positions. What better way to hone my restaurant skills than to start in the front of the house and remind myself of how (or how not) to run a restaurant. I also wanted a work environment that would allow me to loosen up and have more fun than working in an office.

I had already been working in DC and wanted to open a restaurant there so I did an internet search of restaurants in the city that were hiring. The money I could make in the city would also be higher than in Maryland. One posting led me to a hotel rooftop bar that I had never heard of before. I decided to visit in person and inquire about open positions.

The first person I encountered as I stepped off the elevator was Kayla. She was a cute, petite girl with beautiful dark brown skin, full, unruly curls that took over her head and a smile as big as her hair. She energetically asked if I was interested in a table or just heading to the bar. I declined both and asked if she knew whether or not they were hiring. She told me they absolutely were and suggested I apply to be a host since they were short-staffed.

I had hoped to start as a server but she mentioned that they still made pretty good money hourly. She asked for my email address so she could have a manager look out for my online application. At home, I checked out the website and decided to fill out an application for both the host and server positions.

A few days later, I received an automated email that my server application had been denied. I was pretty discouraged until I received an email shortly after to schedule an interview for the host position. Since my schedule was wide open, I set up an interview the very next day.

After waiting in the lobby of the hotel for a few minutes, I was escorted into the indoor area of the restaurant by one of the current host for my interview. As soon as I stepped into the room, I was blown away by the view. They had large floor-to-ceiling windows with views of the Washington Monument. When you walked to the outdoor section, you could see right into the backyard of the White House.

In the corner, there was a black and white chair, reminiscent of the one from *Alice in Wonderland*, facing the window.

As soon as I sat down, a voice arose from behind the chair, "Welcome to your interview." I had no idea what was going on. Was this a prank by one of the employees?

A few seconds later, a woman poked her head from behind the chair and introduced herself as Ricki, the manager I would be interviewing with. She had just been joking around but mentioned how cool it would be to conduct the entire interview that way. We all had a good laugh and once I realized she wasn't crazy, I was able to relax a bit. At least the managers didn't take themselves too seriously and liked to have fun with the staff.

Once it began, the interview was very extensive. There was a list of questions the managers had to ask. Not just the typical 'what would you consider your biggest weakness' questions, but more eccentric ones about fashion, trends, and society, as well as knowledge of liquor and food. The hotel brand the restaurant was located in was very focused on their staff being trendy, young, and fashionable.

Midway through, the director of the restaurant, Ben, came in and introduced himself. He was short but handsome. He gave me a spiel about what he expected from the staff, and I told him I was confident that I would exceed his expectations if hired. I loved everything about the interview and left hoping I would get the job. They told me they would call me in a few days to notify me of their decision.

Mother's Day was approaching so after the interview, I made a stop at Hallmark to grab cards for my mother and grandmother on the way back to my apartment. Whenever I go shopping for my family, I can never stop at one thing. They love little trinkets and collectibles. Angels for my grandmother and bears for my mom are usually safe bets. As I was putting everything into my car, my phone rang.

When I answered, Ricki was on the other side of the phone. "As long as you haven't killed anyone or done any drugs recently, you have the job." Her bizarre antics from the interview continued, but I laughed it off because I needed the job. I didn't mind a quirky boss, it was much better than what I dealt with at my last job.

On my first day, I was greeted again by Kayla. She confessed that she insisted the managers hire me shortly after she met me and I told her how grateful I was that she did. She had such a positive energy, and it was so easy to talk to her. Throughout the day, she walked me around and trained me on what my duties would be. Most of the people I encountered were very welcoming. There were a few servers who seemed pretty standoffish, but I looked to Kayla to give me the rundown on everyone's personalities.

There were two guys who took a particular interest in being very friendly to me during my first few weeks. One was a soft-spoken guy named Brian. He was Hispanic, tall, with a small beer belly and a long beard. He seemed pretty nervous anytime I spoke with him, but he was friends with one of the other hosts who mentioned how nice of a guy he was.

The other guy was named Colin. He was light-skinned, had sleeves of tattoos, curly hair and a baby face. Unlike with Brian, everyone warned me to stay away from him. Not only was he shorter and younger than me, but he had also been in a long-term relationship with one of the servers prior to working there. Even though he always came to the host stand to talk to me, I tried to keep my distance.

Being new, I mostly worked the slower paced day shifts. One evening, while I was gathering my things to head to the metro, Colin stopped me to ask if I minded him walking me out. I replied,

"Don't you have work to do?" He said, "I do whatever I want around here; you'll see." I didn't want to be rude so I said it was fine.

He began to ask me questions about what I liked to do when not at work. I told him my favorite thing to do was travel. Other than that I liked to go out to eat, do some shopping, or watch movies. I liked the simple things. Once we arrived at the entrance of the metro, there was an awkward pause where he looked like he had something to say.

After nothing came out of his mouth, I thanked him for walking with me and turned to leave. A few steps later, he yelled, "Do you mind if I take your number and give you a call?" I knew that was coming. My gut told me it was best to shut down his efforts early on. I had gotten through the first month of keeping him at arm's length off of the advice of most of our coworkers.

He stood there, looking at me with his big, brown eyes and a nervous smile, waiting for my response. After mulling over what harm could come from exchanging numbers with a coworker, I agreed. We did work together. If I rejected him now I would have to face him 5 days a week after that.

Day after day, he continued to come by the host stand and chat with me, but he never called. He did add me on Facebook and start a brief conversation once, but that was our only communication outside of work Maybe he asked for my number just to see if I would say yes.

One evening on my day off, I made plans to meet Jade for dinner. I clicked on her name in my phone log to call her and let her know I was almost at the restaurant. When I selected her name, it began to ring and her picture showed up but a number with a Maryland area code on the screen. I thought that was strange because she had a Virginia phone number, so I hung up immediately. When I clicked on her contact again, the correct number was displayed.

While on the phone with her, another call came in. It was Colin asking if I had just called him. Even though I hadn't, he said he had a missed call from me. I have never been able to figure out how or why but when I called Jade that evening, my phone dialed his phone number. Since we were already on the phone, he took advantage and made conversation.

I asked him why he had never called and he said he could tell I really didn't want to give him my number, so he was waiting until he could talk to me more at work. I told him I was meeting a friend for dinner so I had to go, but before getting off the phone he asked me to go out with him. I told him I would consider meeting up with him the next time we had a day off together.

He told me that when we went out he would pick me up. I preferred driving myself. Even though I appreciated the rare gesture for a man to offer to pick me up, if I wasn't enjoying myself I wanted to be able to leave at my discretion. So I told him to pick a place and I would meet him there.

The following Monday, he convinced me to meet him at the metro stop near my house so he could drive the rest of the way into DC. We arrived at this small, cozy restaurant located on a corner with outdoor seating. As a staff member greeted us at the host stand, he asked to be seated outside.

Once we ordered our drinks and food, the conversation started flowing and I found myself enjoying his company. We had a lot of the same interests and made each other laugh. I was trying my hardest not to like him, but he was slowly chipping away at the wall I'd built up.

After dinner, we didn't want to part ways just yet so we sat in his car like teenagers with the sunroof open, talking while staring up at the stars. It was way past midnight when I finally got out of his car. While at work that same week, he asked me out to dinner again. Even though I could hear the voices of all of the girls at work telling me to say no, I agreed to go out with him again.

Since the only day off we had together was Monday, we met again at the metro and he drove us to a Mexican restaurant I had never heard of before. When we walked in, he gave his name to the host to check-in for his reservation. No guy had ever made a reservation when they took me out before. It was something so simple and basic, but I was impressed.

After waiting at the bar for a few minutes, we were finally seated. It was a struggle to pick out something to eat from the traditional Mexican dishes, but the cocktails were easier to select. By the time we got the check, we had picked over our food but downed four rounds of drinks.

Our second dinner ended the same as the first: sitting in his car, looking at each other and talking the night away. Except that time, he leaned over and kissed me. His lips were so soft and full. We kissed as he tried to pull my body closer to him over the armrest. Even though I kept telling myself I was just going out with him to be nice, deep down I knew I was starting to like him.

Back at work, we pretended as if we barely knew each other to avoid judgment from our coworkers. When I would go into the coat check room, he would sneak in behind me and close the door so we could make out. What he didn't know was that he wasn't the only one who would try to steal kisses in the coat check.

One day when Colin was off, Brian had asked me to hang out with him after work. I tried to politely decline his invitation by saying I didn't have my car to drive where he wanted to go in Virginia. In response, he offered to drive me to the restaurant where he was meeting friends and then drive me back to the city to get on the metro. It seemed as if he really just needed someone to keep him company, so I agreed. During the car ride, he told me things that would normally take months for someone to disclose. When he met me, he felt like I was someone he could trust. I was flattered.

We arrived at a restaurant to hang out with some of his friends and watch a football game. All of his friends were kind and easy to talk to. As we all shared wings, drank beer, and watched football, Brian didn't really pay me much attention. I didn't know if our conversation on the way there made him uneasy or if my reaction wasn't what he was looking for.

Our ride back to the city was much quieter than the way there. That is until he casually mentioned that he wasn't looking for a relationship. That was our first time ever hanging out, and I was already getting the 'don't think this is going anywhere' speech. That comment kind of threw me off. I didn't even know if I liked him yet.

We continued to text and hang out one or two more times outside of work, but he never made any sexual advances towards me. Unless we were at work. Anytime Brian would catch me by myself, whether it be in the coat check, in the storage area, or in the elevator, he would make a move on me. At first, the cat and mouse game we were playing was hot, but then it started to feel weird that he only wanted to hook up at work, where we could possibly get caught. I started telling him I was busy so I couldn't meet up with him.

Once I knew things with Brian were going nowhere, I started to focus more of my attention on Colin. I felt sort of bad about hanging out with both of them without Colin knowing. Brian knew about my relationship with Colin but he didn't care since they weren't close outside of work.

While feeling guilty, I invited Colin over after work one Saturday night. I got off hours before him so in order to stay up, I watched TV and poured myself a drink at my apartment. One drink turned into three so by the time he arrived, I was drunk. He had a few drinks after his shift and brought some alcohol over to share with me. Little did he know I was way ahead of him.

It didn't take long for us to start making out on my couch. Which quickly led to my bedroom. The alcohol I'd consumed may have had some effect on the way I felt but the sex was amazing. Instead of being able to relish in the glory of my sexual satisfaction, I was taken aback by what Colin did next.

We started off using a condom and at some point, he must have thought he was transported to a porn set because he decided to take it off and come all over me and the bed. I was so disgusted that I jumped up immediately. After yelling at him about why he would think doing that was acceptable, I jumped in the shower to wash his semen off me.

Apparently, my response was surprising to him. Everything had gone so well up to that point, but that was a major turn-off. I explained to him, when having sex with someone for the first time, there are certain things he should run by the other person first to make sure it's okay. Ejaculating on them was one of those things.

He looked like a puppy that just peed on the carpet, staring at me wide-eyed with his tail between his legs. He apologized and offered to wash my sheets while we watched TV. At that point, my buzz was wearing off and I was ready to pass out. I ended up falling asleep on the couch until he woke me up to tell me the bed was made.

He asked if I wanted him to leave. Even though the mood had been ruined, I liked having him around. He ended up staying over for the next 2 nights, but we didn't have sex again. I was so traumatized by what happened the first time I pulled away whenever he tried to make a move. I realized we had more to learn about each other.

We were still trying to keep our relationship from everyone we worked with, so for me it became difficult to make the transition from being lovey-dovey outside of work to strangers at work. We were involved in a full-on covert operation. We had to walk to and from work separately, even if we rode there together. I had to duck while in his car if we saw someone we knew approaching. We steered clear of each other at work-related gatherings. We even had each other saved under code names in our phones.

Our production at work combined with some of our coworkers continuing to bash him adversely affected the way I treated him. I was short, irritable, and at times outright mean. There was constantly a battle going on inside of my head on whether to be with him or not.

Being around him made me feel good because he did everything he could to show me how much he liked me. Still, I would only let him in so much. When we would sit on my couch, I didn't want him to touch me; I just wanted him to be there to keep me company. My reactions were equally as confusing and uncomfortable for him.

No matter how standoffish I was, he continued to come over or take me out, so I figured he didn't mind the occasional cold shoulder. Our relationship wasn't able to develop naturally, so it stayed stagnant for months. Until Christmas rolled around.

For the holidays, Colin went out of town to visit family for almost two weeks. While he was gone, I started to miss him more than I thought I would. I realized the way I had been treating him wasn't fair and vowed that when he came back, I was going to change. It took a while but when it was time for spring, I felt like things were on the right track.

We were spending even more time together and after a few months hiatus, we resumed having sex. Things were going well outside of work, but being at work was a different story. His ex-girlfriend, Fiona, was still around and she didn't take the gossip that we were dating well. She would call him late at night or would find reasons to pull him aside to have intimate conversations. Colin would never check her behavior, which caused more problems between us.

Trying to prove he wasn't hiding anything, he made the mistake of giving me the password to his phone. Whenever he would go to the bathroom or leave his phone in the car, I would look at his call log and text messages. I would not only see calls and voicemails from Fiona but text conversations with him flirting with other girls or making plans to hang out.

He and I had yet to decide on being exclusive but after seeing those things in his phone, we needed to have a talk about where things were going. I hadn't been seeing anyone else and since we spent so much time together, I didn't think he was either.

Instead of blowing up on the spot, I would wait and simply ask him if he was talking to other women to see what he would say. He would always respond that he wasn't. After giving him the opportunity to tell truth, which he never took, I would confront him about the conversations I found in his phone. He always had some subpar excuse. "I was just being nice." "We used to hook up a long time ago, but nothing is going on now."

I would try to move past it until his ex-girlfriend called again at 2 AM or I would find new text messages in his phone. Then the fights would start all over again. It was as if he didn't know how to be honest. Since we weren't in a committed relationship there was nothing wrong with him seeing other women until he continued to lie about it. The worst part was that he was a horrible liar and never thought to cover his tracks.

The fact that I couldn't trust him made it hard to see a future between us. By the time summer rolled around, I was reconsidering our relationship altogether. The older I got, the more serious I was about settling down. Since he was younger than me, it didn't seem like he was ready for a serious relationship.

Colin booked a trip to Miami with a few of his friends from college which gave me time to think. While he was there, we didn't talk on the phone much but we texted every day. I tried to give him his space to make bad decisions with his boys. One night, he called me, drunk, telling me how he had been thinking about me the entire time he was on vacation. He wanted to know how I felt about us being in a committed relationship.

Usually, the day a guy wants to make things official is the exact moment a girl hopes for. In this case, the idea of us being in a relationship didn't seem like a good idea. I felt like he was asking me it because it was what he thought I wanted to hear, not because he was actually ready to be committed to me. Until he could be honest with me, the boyfriend title was put on hold.

Had the first six months not been as tumultuous, I would've seriously considered being in a relationship with him. When I told him, I could tell he was disappointed but I assured him it was best to keep things the way they were. We could always revisit the topic later on once we ironed out a few kinks.

After about a year at the restaurant, I transferred to being a server and moved from Maryland to DC in order to be closer to work. Colin ended up staying at my house almost every night. Things between us were consistent. We were getting along better than ever and even scaled back on trying to hide our relationship from everyone at work.

For a few months he had been residing with one of our coworkers. He would always complain about how their smoking would bother him and even though he had his own room, he didn't feel like he had any privacy. Since we had been getting along so well and he was at my house every night anyway, I made a suggestion that was probably the worst thing for our relationship at its unsettled state: he should move in with me.

We weren't at the place in our relationship where we should've been living together but at the time, it made sense. He was paying so much money for a room that he never stayed in. Helping me out financially wasn't a stipulation for him to move in, but he offered to pay 300 dollars a month towards the bills.

Gradually, he began to bring his clothes over and stored his larger furniture at his parents' house. I cleared out a teeny tiny space in my closet for him and brought him a temporary storage unit because I had way too many clothes to offer him a drawer. Once he moved everything in, we settled into a comfortable routine.

We would go grocery shopping together, and he would cook breakfast for me and I would cook dinner for him. He was always offering to rub my feet or preparing baths with Epsom salt for me to soak in after work. It also became convenient to ride to work in the same car, so we saved on gas each week. Living together seemed to do us well, but the good times didn't last for long.

Shortly after his first full month of living with me, I still hadn't received the money he offered to pay. I was uncomfortable asking him about it so I just waited, hoping he would bring it up. I knew he had a lot of debt and was still helping his roommate cover the rent since he moved out so abruptly. So I let the first month go by without saying a word.

Then the same thing happened the next month, and the month after that. I couldn't ignore the elephant in the apartment any longer. While watching TV one night, I asked him if he remembered that he said he would contribute financially before he moved in. If he didn't plan on doing it, he shouldn't have offered. Over time I ended up buying the groceries myself unless he came with me, which was never, on top of paying rent and utilities while he lived there taking advantage of all of the amenities.

He told me his money was tight but the next time he got paid, he would start helping out. More time passed and I had only received half of what he said he would pay for one month. I was so frustrated by him constantly failing to live up to what he said he was going to do that everything else he did began to irritate me.

I couldn't stand to see him constantly run water to wash dishes or leave the lights on when he left a room. My lifestyle was all about finding ways to reduce my carbon footprint. My top priority was recycling everything possible, turning off and unplugging things that weren't being used as much as possible, and to reduce the amount of energy or resources I used. Colin, on the other hand, wasn't as concerned about the environment, or cleanliness for that matter.

Whenever he would brush his teeth, there would be water marks all over the sink and the mirror. He would shed and leave his curly hair, from whichever part of his body, all over the bathroom. When he came in the house, he would gradually undress, leaving his clothes everywhere. He didn't mind washing dishes or making the bed, but the rest of the apartment was left for me to clean including washing his clothes. I felt like more of a caretaker than a girlfriend.

There was nothing he did that didn't get on my nerves. Since we were together all of the time, there was no time for me to decompress. He no longer took me out on dates; he found it more convenient to sit on the couch, watch movies, and order takeout pizza or Chinese food. None of my clothes fit because he had a habit of getting McDonald's almost every day.

While working at the ATF, I had lost 10 pounds by watching what I ate. Pre-Colin, I ate low-calorie prepackaged meals and cooked healthy dinners in combination with cutting out fast food. Post-Colin, the most we cooked at home was waffles, eggs, and bacon for breakfast or chicken fingers and fries for dinner.

Months of frustration about everything he ever did that bothered me had built up. While he was in the bathroom, I decided to do a quick scan of his phone and found a recent message where he was practically begging to take a girl out to eat. All of that time had passed where I thought we were rebuilding our relationship but instead he was still fucking around behind my back. If was still trying to pursue other women over text while we were in the same room together, I didn't want to imagine what he was doing when he went out with his friends.

When he returned to the room, I waited a few minutes then asked him again if he was talking to any other females. Of course, he said no. So I asked, "If that's the case, can I see your phone?" He agreed to hand it over but before he did, I saw him pressing way too many buttons. When I asked what he was doing, he said, "Nothing" and handed me the phone. As I looked through his text messages, two conversation I had seen minutes before were missing.

Not only did he lie about talking to other women but as he deleted their conversation right in front of my face, he lied again. Nothing had changed other than our living situation. I told him I had already seen what he just deleted and gave him another opportunity to explain himself. He tried backtracking and lying even more, but I cut him off because it pained me to see him try to lie his way out.

Either he was going to stop being dishonest or he needed to move out. He agreed to do better but he also made me promise to stop going through his phone. I told him if he didn't have anything to hide then it wouldn't matter but I told him I would stop. I still did it from time to time, I just no longer directly confronted him about it.

He began to switch up his routine and started going out to clubs and drinking more. Our nights of going to the movies or relaxing on the couch together were replaced with him coming home late, drunk off of peach Cîroc. It really bothered me that even if he had no one to go with, he felt the need to be out drinking all night by himself.

Since I was only issued one key fob to get into my apartment building, I would have to get up in the middle of the night to go downstairs and let him in. It wasn't like he was going out every once in a while; it would be two or three times every single week. Getting a good night's sleep became few and far between.

Whenever he did go out, he would get drunk to excess, which also included him driving home drunk. I couldn't say I had never done it, but not to the extent he did. I would repeatedly tell him to call me if he was too drunk to drive because I would rather come get him than risk him getting into an accident or getting pulled over. He never listened.

One morning, we both had to work an early shift and decided to take his truck. I walked up to the passenger side and noticed major damage to the front. When I asked him what happened, he had no recollection of hitting his car. That was one of the times where he was blackout drunk and still decided to drive home.

Being so drunk and going out all the time was a major turn-off. Those nights usually ended up in him peeing somewhere he wasn't supposed to or causing damage to my property or his. It began to drive a wedge between us. Add to that months of him being late to pay his portion of the bills, not helping out around the house, and constantly being caught in lies. Our already unstable relationship began to deteriorate.

Since it bothered me that he desired to spend his nights in the club instead of with me, we began to argue about not spending enough time together. To him, the time we spent simply being in the same room together was quality time. However, I wanted us to try new things, take trips, or even do a staycation in DC. I was constantly pleading with him to plan something special for us to do outside of the usual movies and dinner. He promised he would, but nothing would ever come of it.

After months of feeling like I was the only one working at our relationship, I knew things weren't going to work out. I no longer felt like I was a priority to him. Just because he succeeded at getting me to fall for him didn't mean he could stop putting in effort after he got me. In a relationship, there were so many expectations that he wasn't even close to meeting.

As time went on, the distance between us grew no matter how close we were in proximity. I became insecure about why he never made an effort to make me feel important. My self-esteem dropped as I tried to figure out why I wasn't worth the effort. I also no longer felt good about the way I looked since I had gained so much weight.

I thought long and hard about whether our relationship was something worth holding on to any longer. After coming to the conclusion Colin and I had run its course, I asked him to move out. He made plans to move back in with his former roommate and packed all of his things that same day. He moved out all of his clothes first and informed me he would come back for his electronics.

As he moved throughout the apartment, putting his belongings into bags, I just sat on the couch watching him, not saying a word. My face was directed at the TV but my eyes were watching his every move. He didn't apologize for anything, try to redeem himself, or say goodbye; he just situated all of his bags on the dolly and closed the door.

At first, I was relieved. Our relationship had become such a dark time that when he left it gave light more room to shine. Then I looked around my bedroom and it felt empty and cold. As soon as I sat down on the bed, I began to sob uncontrollably. I rubbed my hand over the side he always slept on, knowing he wasn't going to be sleeping there with me every night anymore. I laid down and continued to cry for the rest of the afternoon, mourning the end of a relationship I had spent two of my prime dating years on.

When he returned for the rest of his things, we sat down and tried to have a conversation about why our relationship was never on the right track. While all of his lying and perceived neglect took a toll on me, he confessed that the rejection I showed him early on, especially when he asked me to be his girlfriend, had negatively affected him. It never occurred to me that even though holding off on being in a committed relationship at the time was the right thing to do, it had caused him to resent me all that time.

We had never been on the same page. In the beginning, he pulled out all the stops to break down my walls and ease my hesitation to date him. He made me feel like I was a prize he had won and always showed me how much he appreciated me giving him a chance. But from the beginning, he felt like his efforts were unappreciated, so his walls began to go up as mine were coming down.

As soon as something shifted for me and I started to see a future with him, he began to pull away. The roles had reversed, and then I started doing all of the work to get him to invest in our relationship. Maybe it was my fault for letting other people get into my head and not following my heart, but at least I was always honest with him about how I felt.

Throughout our relationship Colin would hold his feelings in instead of working through what was wrong, which resulted in him putting in less effort. I could sense that he wasn't happy, but he would never tell me why. Frequently, things would go well for weeks, then when I least expected it, he would explode on me about all of the things I did that bothered him. I would be left confused and blindsided.

Even though our relationship had many peaks and valleys, we had become best friends in the process. I was the first person he could tell his radical thoughts to that he felt other people would judge him for. With him, I could be vulnerable, spoiled, and childish, behavior that I would be embarrassed to show anyone else. We had seen each other at our best and our worst.

We were so used to doing everything together that after a few months apart we began to hang out again. Generally our communication would resume after I would receive a "You up?" text and subsequent phone call when he was drunk. After several tries I would give in and he would end up back at my apartment.

The back and forth went on for another year after he moved out. Our problem was that we never addressed the issues that caused us to split in the first place. Even though I would let him back in, he didn't change. Every time I would try to talk to him about something that was bothering me he would dismiss my feelings and tell me I was overreacting.

One source of tension was a particular girl who used to work at the restaurant before I started. Whenever she saw him, she liked to hang all over him and leave lipstick kisses on the side of his face. To him, since he didn't have feelings for her, it wasn't a big deal. I tried to explain to him that regardless of his intentions, I felt like her behavior was disrespectful and it bothered me that he refused to address it with her.

Other sources of tension involved him planning events with his friends for a holiday or at a club without telling me. I would have to hear about it from people at work. Since he felt comfortable telling everyone at work, why not tell the person he was lying next to in bed every night?

Then there were the pet names and special favors he would do for certain female coworkers. He made the mistake of telling me which girls from work he found attractive so every time he was around them, I would pay close attention to the way he reacted. There would be times where he would be having a conversation with a girl and it was almost as if I didn't exist. The words 'babe' and 'sweetie' were thrown around way too often.

There were so many little things he did that bothered me and without resolution, they turned into big issues. His constant dismissal of my concerns or his typical "I don't understand why you're mad" comments began to weigh on me. He felt like no matter he did, he never had a reason to apologize because his intent wasn't to make me upset.

Out of the blue, after what seemed like an eternity of disappointment, he finally took the initiative and suggested we spend the night together at a local hotel. Even though the weather was horrible due to a tropical storm, I couldn't pass up the first opportunity for us to go to a hotel after dating for two years.

There were so many things I wanted us to do together and that had been one of them. I felt like it was the beginning of him showing me that he was reinvested in our relationship. We stayed in the room all night, ordered room service, and splurged on pay-per-view movies. It was such a romantic and fun night.

The next morning, I headed home and he headed to work. During the day, I didn't hear from him much, but I figured that was because work was busy. We were both supposed to go out that night for a coworker's birthday. Since I knew I would see him later I didn't reach out, confident things would pick back up from where we left them at the hotel.

Instead, I was greeted by a standoffish Colin who really didn't say much the entire night. At no point did he make an effort to be near me. Because of things being so tense between us, I was distracted from having fun. Instead of allowing my sour mood to bring others down or getting into it with him at a club, I decided to leave. I was confused about why he was acting so differently after we had just spent a great night together. I couldn't think of anything I did to upset him.

As I was walking to my car, Colin came up behind me. He approached me and said he could tell I was upset inside the club. I asked him what his deal was and why he was being so distant. He told me he had spent the entire day at work trying to figure out how he was feeling about our relationship. The words seemed to be stuck in his throat, so I asked him to elaborate.

Every time we talked about what his problem was, there was a different reason. I felt myself getting more and more upset. The issues he had were so vague that I finally asked him, "Why are you wasting my time?" All I wanted was the honest truth; I couldn't keep doing the back-and-forth anymore. It seemed like as soon as things were going good and we were getting more serious, he would suddenly have a reason to pull away.

The reasons he gave me were baseless and I disputed every one of them. No, I wasn't trying to pressure him to marry me and be the father of my kids. No, I didn't have a desire to see other people. No, I didn't wish he was more successful or established. I felt like he was putting his insecurities on me, trying to make me feel like I was the cause of the pressure he was feeling.

I was determined to get the real reason out of him as to why he kept pulling away. He finally blurted out, "Because I want the option to date other people." I could feel a lump forming in my throat as my eyes began to burn. For several months, every time I asked him if he was dating other women, his response was always the same: he had no desire to date anyone else.

He went so far as to tell me he hadn't even gotten a single phone number during the time we were together. Instead of being honest about his desire to play the field, he kept trying to project that desire onto me. He repeatedly told me he felt like I should see other people because he couldn't give me everything I wanted. He wanted me to know he would be supportive if I found someone else who could give me all the things he couldn't. All because he really wanted the freedom to sleep with other women.

I turned down numerous advances from men and shied away from meeting new guys because I made him a priority. I constantly reassured him that he was enough for me, even though deep down I didn't truly believe it. Over time, I began to degrade my positive attributes and successes to stroke his ego and make him feel less insecure. I would make excuses for feeling unhappy and unsatisfied with the way I was being treated because I believed that eventually he would do right by me.

As things began to come back into focus around me, I wished that I could erase the last two and half years of my life. I told him he was incapable of being honest, almost as if he was a pathological liar. All of the time he spent denying the real reasons why he didn't want to be in a committed relationship with me, he was blocking me from achieving the healthy and supportive relationship I desired with someone else. I got in my car and pulled off. I wanted to get away from him as quickly as I could.

I looked in my rear view mirror and could see him walking towards his car. It was hard to let go, but I needed to stop thinking he would change after he'd showed me repeatedly that he wasn't going to. I pledged to myself that was the last time I was going to try and figure out why we couldn't work.

Even though it was 4 AM when I finally arrived at my apartment, I went through every room and got rid of everything that reminded me of him. There would not be a single thing left behind that might compel me to reach out to him. I went around collecting his toothbrush, the house shoes, body wash, and hair products I bought him along with the food that only he ate. It all went in the trash can.

I finished the night by changing my sheets and washing my

comforter to get rid of any traces of his scent. The clothes he left behind went into a bag for a clothing donation. The bracelet he gave me I put in my work bag to give to a coworker who had been admiring it. I combed over every inch of my apartment to get rid of the slightest trace that he was ever there.

The one thing I couldn't get rid of were the memories of the time we spent there together. There was nothing I could do to get rid of all of those thoughts that came to mind when I looked around my apartment. No matter how much I purged.

The next day, I had to go to work and put on a brave face for the guests and my coworkers, even though I wanted to burst into tears. I didn't feel like talking about how hurt I was. There were only a few girls at work who knew how much I had gone through in my relationship with Colin. Still, I didn't go into too much detail because I would have lost it during my shift.

By spending more time with my family over the next few days, my mind was too distracted to be depressed. Celebrating my mom's birthday forced me to put a smile on my face, cheer up, and act like nothing was wrong. I allowed myself to indulge in tons of home-cooked food and a little too much cake. After a breakup, carbs made me feel better.

While at work, my goal was to continue carrying on the charade that I had it all together. When our shift was over, it was common for some of the staff to go out for drinks at Harry's Bar and Grill, since it was one block away and the entire staff was treated like VIP. During my Saturday night shift, I could feel myself falling apart, so I decided to leave before everyone else to fit in a few drinks before last call.

One of the hostesses, Kerry, was already off and met me at the bar. As we sat together for over an hour, I waited for her to ask me, even once, how I was doing. Instead, she spent the entire time complaining about work and her roommates. I sat there and stared at my reflection in the mirror behind the bar, wondering if anyone truly cared about how I was doing.

We closed out our tab and walked towards the main road so she could catch a cab and I could head to my car. As we approached the street and she continued to go on and on about her superficial problems, I stopped walking and screamed at her, "No one ever asks me how I'm doing!" I couldn't hold in how I was feeling anymore. I hadn't talked to anyone about the demise of my relationship with Colin, and I felt like I was going to explode.

She turned back with a look of confusion on her face. "What's wrong, babe? You seem like you're doing so well, so I didn't think anything was wrong." I had done such a successful job of hiding in plain sight at work that no one could tell I needed a shoulder to cry on.

Outside of those walls, I needed to vent, needed to talk, and needed someone to care. Whenever something was wrong, I would always call on Colin to help me feel better. But who was going to console me about him? The girls at work I was close with were so blissfully happy in their own relationships that I didn't want to burden them with my constant failures and missteps. Making the same mistakes over and over with the same guy gets old to talk about after a while.

Kerry repeatedly asked me what was going on but I was so embarrassed by my outburst that I just wanted to get in my car and cry in solitude. She pushed me into a corner and held me there until I started talking. Once the first few words left my lips, I couldn't stop the tears from flowing out of my eyes.

I divulged how much effort I put into keeping my relationship with Colin intact and how worthless I felt that he never really appreciated me. He constantly told me how important I was to him but if that was the case, why did he do so many things to hurt me? Why was I not enough? The way my dating history had gone it made me feel like I was never going to find love. I was always going to be left hurt and disappointed.

After crying and talking with Kerry in the entryway of a closed business for half an hour, two servers from work, Hannah and Erica, walked by on their way to the parking garage. I saw them look over at us but they continued walking. A few moments later, they came back to see what was wrong.

I explained why I rushed out of work and what I had been going through, which resulted in me crying all over again. For as long as we were together I kept most of his wrongdoings to myself. Everyone would always comment about what a great guy he was and he was great, if you didn't have to date him.

I was tired of holding in everything that had been going wrong for years and how unhappy I was. For so long, I had been highlighting all of my flaws and downplaying my attributes because Colin constantly made comments about what he couldn't offer or his shortcomings. In order to make him feel like more of a man, I would say that having my own house, own car, and great credit really weren't all that great.

Not feeling heard or understood led me to feel irrational and unreasonable because he refused to understand how he hurt me. After days of mulling over what I said or consulting with his friends, he would change his tune. Simply because what I said in the first place received validation from his peers.

I longed for someone I could have serious talks with about

marriage and having kids, but he wasn't that guy. Talking about the future made him uncomfortable. If I ever mentioned how cute a baby was or talking about someone's engagement, he felt like I was pressuring him to propose.

Even though he would fight with me, he wouldn't fight *for* me. We were constantly arguing about the lack of effort he put into our relationship. There were so many times he would mention a new activity for us to do but never followed through. Eventually, I got used to his minimal effort. If he did something once, he would reference that for several months as proof that he made an effort.

When we did do anything other than dinner and movies, it would be because I planned it. Then I noticed a pattern emerge where a few days before I had something planned for us—such as a concert, a trip, or an outing with other couples—he would start an argument. I always felt like he was sabotaging anything I organized.

Our relationship may have been successful if it was built on a more solid foundation. Instead I started a relationship with a guy dozens of people told me was wrong for me. We went from me being distant to him being a liar. Then instead of ending a relationship that didn't make either of us happy, we dragged it out because we were comfortable.

Had he sat down and looked at the core of what I was asking for, it was very simple: for him to be honest, respectful, communicate better, and treat me as if he valued me in his life. If he was honest about what he wanted out of our relationship early on then I would've had all of the facts to make an informed decision to stay with him or move on.

As soon as he felt unsure about whether he was ready to handle everything that came along with being in a committed relationship, he should've shared that with me. Not drag the situation out for months letting me think we were working towards something real. He always knew he wasn't ready, but I guess he was either afraid of losing me altogether or afraid to tell me the truth.

With all that I blamed him for, I was by no means easy to deal with. I was moody, impatient, presumptuous, and at times extremely emotional and demanding. I had nasty habits of jumping to conclusions, bringing up the past, and having selective hearing. However, unlike him, I was actually making an effort to work on the things that bothered him.

Although our relationship helped me grow and recognize things I needed to change about myself, I felt like I had wasted my prime dating years. In your 20s, you go into relationships with the goal that it will develop into something long lasting and substantial. That wasn't what Colin was looking for and deep down he knew it from the moment he first asked me to give him a chance.

From that moment on I needed to trust my intuition and see the signs as they presented themselves that a man wasn't a good fit for me, instead of hoping he will turn into something he's not ready to be. I settled for less than I deserved for far too long. The more time passed and the older I got, it was harder to walk away. I had invested so much time, effort and emotion into our relationship; I didn't want to look back at the years I spent with him and have nothing to show for it.

In the end, wasting time on something that wasn't working was worse than being alone. Instead of letting him go and finding a man who cherished me like I was the best thing that ever happened to him or finding happiness with myself I tried to fix something that didn't want to be fixed. I had no more time to spend feeling unsure, unloved, and unwanted. A commitment from a man would never be worth breaking that commitment to myself.

CHAPTER 12

2014

As I sat on the couch in my living room, staring out into the back yard of the home I purchased by myself, I was proud of what I had accomplished by the age of 28. I had a job that allowed me to live a comfortable life. I traveled as much as I could to explore other states and countries. I was in good health with a great group of friends and a loving family. I lived a blessed life. Despite all of that, my love life was one disappointment after the next.

If there was an advisor for relationships, as there were for investments, mine would advise me to stop investing in such high-risk, low-return men. When it came to other people's relationships, I could clearly see the mistakes they were making. When it came to me, I made so many poor choices, usually the same ones over and over hoping for a different result. There were so many times I felt undeserving of being treated with respect and value. So many lies I turned a blind eye to, big or small. I put my wants and needs on the back burner to prioritize men who weren't deserving.

In the seven years since I sat on the couch in Jaime's office, I was still struggling to implement the lessons I learned. When I heard her voice say that I had to stop settling for crumbs I would silence it because I didn't want to end up alone. The pressure of turning 30 soon weighed on me. The older I got, the more I felt like I had to let go of some of my expectations.

Everywhere I looked, people were getting engaged, walking down the aisle to marital bliss, or having babies. Then there were the comments from my grandparents about how they wished they had a baby around the house. They were such loving people and I knew they couldn't wait to spoil my kids. My biggest fear was that it would take me so long to have kids that they wouldn't have enough time with them. With me being an only child and my mom and uncle declaring they were too old to have kids, all of the pressure was on me.

So many fears about not being able to find everything I wanted in one man kept me fighting for mediocre and unfulfilling relationships. If I wasn't with the man of my dreams already, maybe I was never going to meet him. So I had to make do with the options that were available to me.

While people-watching at work or out with friends in social settings there weren't a lot of eligible black men to choose from. It never failed that they fell into one of three eliminating factors. Either they were already in a relationship, gay, or they weren't interested in black women.

I am a firm believer that there should be no restriction on who anyone dates. We are all entitled to have preferences on the appearance of who we are interested in dating. However, I noticed that every attractive, well-mannered black man I would spot would only approach women with fair complexions. It actually made me sad when I went out because I was never going to have fair skin or naturally straight hair so I was never going to be of interest to those men.

I wanted to be an equal-opportunity dater but the more I

learned about the world, black history, and seeing the way black people were being treated in my country, I gained so much pride and respect being black.

Deep in my heart, my desire was to marry a black man and eventually create equally-as-proud black children. With the treatment and perception of black men being what it was, I wanted to stand by black men as much as I could. Unfortunately, the black men I encountered didn't reciprocate the sentiment.

Two of my best friends, Elaine and Laurel, had both found black men to settle down with, so all hope wasn't lost. During my dating process, I had to filter through the men who wanted to have sex on the first night, expected me to chase them, or guys who would pull a disappearing act.

Most men didn't know how to court women. It was no longer them picking you up, opening doors, and doing things just because to make women feel special. Instead they were slapping women's asses, texting instead of calling, and first dates consisted of sitting on the couch.

It seemed like every guy I met was playing a game I didn't have the right codes to. Was I supposed to do more or less? Was I supposed to put it all out there or hold back? Was I supposed to play hard to get or make things easy?

At one time or another, I sat back and listened to my family and friends tell me how beautiful and amazing I was, with all of these wonderful attributes. After every romantic failure, they would rally around me, saying, "He's out there! Don't get down!" No matter how many times I heard it, I began to lose the desire to keep trying.

I wanted a guy who didn't play games or disappear for days at a time. I wanted to know that I was on his mind. When he made plans, he would actually follow through with them. I wouldn't have to deal with excuses about why he didn't call or text back or why we didn't see each other.

A large part of my problem stemmed from the kind of guys I was attracted to. I had progressed past the jerks I chased when I was a teenager but my eyes were still drawn to the most physically attractive guys in the room. The problem was every other woman in the room was after them too.

When men have the luxury of options when dating, they're less likely to want to give that up by settling down. Especially with there being so many beautiful women in the Washington DC area. The city was overflowing with women of different ethnicities, body types, hair types, hair lengths, and various exotic features.

If guys did approach me, they were never the older, professionally dressed men I was attracted to. I would get the younger, immature guys using inappropriate jokes as their opening line. They were the ones with a wandering eye I would see talking to another girl three seconds after they walked away from me.

I wasn't looking to have fun and play around; I was looking for substance, and they had 'only here for hookups' written all over their face. There were so many guys who had never respected or understood the word commitment.

There was a very small selection of eligible men in DC who were attractive, educated, employed, and independent. The older you got, the more you felt like you had to compromise on the traits you desired in order to find a significant other. Not to mention if you weren't willing to do what a guy wanted when he wanted it, there was another woman waiting for the opportunity to pick up the slack.

We as women also made it harder on ourselves. There were so many who allowed guys to treat them disrespectfully, put an easy pass on getting in their pants, and held such low standards for men that when a woman *with* standards came along, men were unwilling to rise to meet them. Why work for the time and affection of a woman when there were 10 other ones who didn't require as much effort?

No matter their shortcomings in the beginning, men would turn on the charm to reel you in and then gradually show their true intentions. All women were susceptible to falling for an asshole or player because of the charm they possessed, each one of them proven to be emotionally unavailable.

In my mind, I felt like I had been single my entire life. I had yet to experience a supportive, functioning, long-term, committed relationship. Regardless of what title I had with Colin, I wanted to strike our relationship from my dating record because I felt like it had been based on fraud.

In the kind of relationship I desired, I would have been treated like a queen. My man would value me, share pride in all of my accomplishments, big or small, and do everything in his power to protect me from heartache or pain. My goal was to be with someone who shared my desire to do everything possible to make the other feel loved, safe, and encouraged. Someone who could envision building a future together.

Too often I lost sight of what was possible and got lost in what was available in that moment. I was afraid of seeming high-maintenance or needy so there were times when I didn't hold men to the highest standard. I compromised what I wanted, lowered my expectations, and put up with the wrong kind of attention. As a willing participant in my dating blunders, I couldn't sit around and say all men were to blame or pretend like I was always blindsided when things didn't work out.

At my job, I was surrounded by extremely beautiful women of all shapes, backgrounds, and ethnicities who were smart, funny, independent, and completely deserving of being swept off of their feet. No matter what made us different, in the end we all had shared the same experience in dealing with disappointing men.

All of us could relate to being cheated on, lied to, led on, or having a guy tell us he wasn't ready for commitment then see him in a relationship with another girl in a matter of weeks. No matter how optimistic we were in the beginning about the guy we met at a club, restaurant, or through a friend, the courtship generally ended on a sour note.

There were a handful of girls who were happy in long-term relationships. The rest of us single girls constantly endured numerous dry and empty dates. Some of us battled with unhealthy on-and-off relationships with the same guy spanning months or years, struggling to break free and give ourselves the chance to see what else was out there.

It was easier to go back to unhealthy situations that were comfortable instead of dealing with the uncertainty of someone new. Whenever a moment arose where we were lonely, bored, or drunk, we would fall back into old habits. Sometimes I couldn't keep up with the relationship drama going on with people at work. One week a girl would be single, the next week she would be back with the guy who broke her heart, and then a few weeks later there would be a new guy she was excited about.

Every time I met a new guy and it didn't work out, I vowed to give up on dating. Which each date I had to learn all of their likes and dislikes. I had to get used to their personality and sense of humor, then figure out what offends them. In turn, they had to do the same for me. Being as sensitive as I was, it was easy for me to cut someone off based on a rude comment or joke.

Phone etiquette was the worst part. If a guy didn't call me first I figured he must not be interested, but really they were expecting me to call. Did people even talk on the phone anymore, or was it acceptable to just text and never hear the person's voice again until the first date? If I texted or called them, how long was I supposed to wait for a response? When were we supposed to make plans to see each other? If too much time passed without him making an effort to see me, should I not answer the next time I hear from him?

I also had to navigate dating in a world run by social media. Everyone wanted to know my Facebook or Instagram handle before even asking what my hobbies were. On the other hand, I would meet people who already knew things about me because we were 'friends' online but I had no clue who they were. How much information was too much at first?

My desire was for things to go back to the way they were when my grandparents met. My grandfather walked into a diner with his Army buddies where my grandmother happened to be serving at the time. He tipped her a quarter (which was big money back then) and then came back to that same restaurant to pursue her.

There were no games, no mystery about his intentions, no codes to unlock in order to get to the first date. A man saw a woman he was interested in and he courted her. He opened doors, he picked her up to take her out, he called her phone at respectable hours, and he put in the effort necessary to win her over. I wanted things to be traditional when it came to dating.

I wanted to hold out for the guy who would see me in a

room and say to himself, "I have to talk to her." He would call me the next day, not a week later. After making reservations for dinner, he would pick me up with flowers in hand. As much as I loved flowers, only three men had given me flowers in my entire life and one was my grandfather.

While dating I wanted to receive a good morning text me to let me know he was thinking about me or a call before going to bed. Not a 'you up' text at 1 in the morning. I would receive gifts on days that weren't my birthday, a holiday or special occasion. We would have weekend getaways, take trips all over the world, and created memories together. Relationships weren't solidified in a day. They required endless time, effort, and compromise to thrive. With hard work, relationships were rewarding.

My friends, coworkers, and even my mom would share with me similar horror stories about men. Every time another guy grabbed my ass in the club, didn't call me back, or made me pay for my own movie ticket, I just kept telling myself it was just one more frog I had to endure to make me appreciate my Prince Charming that much more.

Relationships, like a sandwich, needed more than a shell to be classified as such. In order to call something a sandwich, there's an ingredient other than bread. Whether it's filled with meat, vegetables, condiments, or for some people chips, there's some sort of substance. That's what I wanted—a man who would do everything to make my heart full, not leave me feeling empty with unfulfilled promises.

Since two of my best friends were in healthy, supportive, and loving relationships, I knew what I sought was possible. They both were blessed to find men who adored and cherished them. The lengths they would go to make each other happy warmed my heart. No relationship was perfect, but they each worked hard to make the other person happy. No matter what disagreements they had, their love for each other was stronger than any squabble. As their friend, I was happy for the love they found, but being around them always reminded me of how far away I was from experiencing that for myself.

Always being the third or fifth wheel could get old, even though we always had a good time hanging out together. While hearing stories of couple's trips, romantic gestures, how they took care of each other when they were sick and the surprises they planned for each other, I would think to myself, why couldn't I have that? On the other hand, it made it easier to get over Colin because it reminded me of all the things he didn't do.

My grandmother constantly reassured me that the right man was out there for me, but I always told her, "Don't get your hopes up." Deep down in the core of my being, I felt like finding true love wasn't meant for me.

In my early twenties, I had high hopes of being a young mom with at least 2 kids in a house full of love and laughter that I built with the man I had planned to spend the rest of my life with. I saw myself working a 9-to-5 office job, going to all of my kids' school and extracurricular activities, and then coming home to make dinner for my family. We can never plan the course our lives are going to take, but I had high hopes it was the life I would be living by the time I reached 28. Even though none of that panned out for me, I had so much to be grateful for.

On almost a daily basis, I found myself with baby fever and man envy. Everywhere I looked, people were having babies and falling in love. It was a constant fight to not less pessimism and bitterness win. All of the romantic movies I thought would inspire me ended up making me feel even worse. In the end, the girl always found love. At first, it gave me hope that there was some man out there, just like the character in the movie, ready to sweep me off my feet. After every horrible dating experience, I knew the guys I saw on the big screen were just trying to sell me a dream.

My friend Nicki was the only person from college and my sorority I kept in touch with. We would meet about once a month for brunch or dinner to catch up and talk about everything from men to the girls we knew from college. We were both unlucky in love and found solace in sharing our experiences.

We would go over the girls from college who were one by one getting married and having babies. She would receive invites to each wedding and baby shower while I only saw the photos afterwards on Facebook. She spent her early twenties focusing on school and I spent my early twenties focusing on losers, so by our late twenties we were raising the white flag and racking our brains trying to find new ways to meet eligible bachelors.

Every time I went out and returned home with no potential prospects, I would lose interest in going out at all. The effort it took to get dressed up and do my makeup then spend money on gas, parking, drinks, and food didn't seem worth it. By the end of the night, I would be shoved or bumped into dozens of times, my dress and shoes were soiled from drinks being spilled on me, and to top it off, my feet were in pain from wearing heels.

The less faith I had in finding true love, the more I faced the reality that I may have to consider accomplishing my goals on my own. I wasn't getting any younger, and I wanted to try to have kids before the challenges of trying to conceive at an older age made it impossible. It was also extremely important to me for my children to know the amazing love and support my grandparents had to offer. Their mortality was becoming very real to me.

I knew there were plenty of women who had healthy children later on in life, but I didn't want to wait. I wanted to be able to relate to my kids, to run and play with them and have as many years with them as I could before my health declined.   My mom had me at a young age and we ended up being best friends. That was the kind of relationship I desired to have with my children. If I waited too late, I would end up being the older, out-of-touch, embarrassing mom her kids didn't want to be seen with.

As unreasonable or rash the idea may have seemed, having a kid on my own was becoming a very strong possibility. I didn't need a man to help my buy a house, a car, or manage my bank accounts; maybe I didn't need one to have a baby either. Was I simply being impatient and irrational, or was this my only option as a result of wasting so much time on the wrong guys in the past?

I knew the challenges I would face being a single mother because of how my mom had to sacrifice so much to make sure I had everything I needed. Although we lived with my grandparents for some of my childhood, my mom was solely financially responsible for taking care of me. She always worked two jobs to provide for me, which didn't leave much time to do things for herself.

Her focus was always to make sure I didn't want for anything. She didn't get back into the habit of getting her nails and hair done consistently until I was an adult. She had also remained single for most of my life, which I felt partially responsible for. She focused so much of her free time on me that it didn't leave a lot of time for dating.

Even though we had our challenges and I didn't have the childhood other kids at my school had, I wouldn't change a single thing. I owe any success and accomplishments I've achieved to the dedication, love, and support of my mother. But even though she did an amazing job raising me on her own, single motherhood was never going to be easy.

Had I made better decisions on who I dated maybe I would've been married with two kids already. I believed every decision was significant. Life is made up of a series of choices, and whichever one you choose has a domino effect on everything that happens from that point on.

If you decide to stop in a store instead of walking straight, you could miss running into someone at the next corner. If you decide to take a back route instead of the highway, you could avoid an accident. There have been so many times where I've said to myself "Only if I had gone there first" or "Only if I had left two minutes earlier". Once those decisions have been made, whether they were the best choice or not, there's nothing we can do to alter what happens afterwards.

Thinking back on the misguided decisions I made when I was younger got me thinking about rebuilding relationships I had lost. Life was too short not to say what was on my mind or to have regrets. There were some relationships where I regretted how they ended, so I sought those individuals out to make amends. Most of the time, it boiled down to simple miscommunication and the realization that whatever went wrong wasn't worth losing someone forever.

The first person who came to mind was Ella. She and I were great friends for five years. She even moved in with me and my mom for a few months when she first moved to Maryland. She was a free-spirited singer who wasn't afraid to get up and move wherever her heart desired. I admired her independence and resilience.

After leaving Maryland, she moved to Florida for a few months and then New York. I visited her once in New York to see her perform at an underground club. She was so unique, confident,

charismatic, and everyone loved her raspy voice. Her drive
motivated me to consider taking artistic risks in my own life. She
never cared what anyone thought and lived her life the way she
wanted to, regardless of the opinion of others.

While living in New York, she met a musician from Paris
and quickly fell head over heels. After seeing pictures of him, I didn't
blame her. He looked like a model with tan skin, long blond hair,
and an athletic build. It only took a few months after meeting him
for her to pick up and follow him to Paris.

She claimed that she didn't move there for him but instead
to hone her skills as a musician, even though New York had a
significant network of established and independent musicians. I was
amazed she moved so far away from everything she knew, especially
with no knowledge of France or its language.

Before heading across the Atlantic Ocean, she invited me
to come visit her in Paris for her birthday. With her birthday being
right before Thanksgiving, it would've been the first holiday I didn't
spend with my family. On top of that, I didn't know any French
other than "*Oui*", so it was a lot to consider.

After checking for flights, I took a leap of faith and booked
my trip before the fares climbed any higher. It was the chance of a
lifetime to travel to such a beautiful and iconic place in Europe. The
flight wasn't terribly expensive, and I rationalized the fact that I
could stay with Ella for free, so in all, it was worth it for such a
priceless experience.

In preparing for the trip, I felt like Carrie Bradshaw in the
final episodes of *Sex and the City*. Everything I was too self-conscious
to wear at home, I packed to wear in Paris. It was going to be cold
and rainy there, but I didn't care. Missing my first family

Thanksgiving was the only thing that concerned me, since it was my grandfather's favorite holiday, but my family understood.

My mom dropped me off at the airport for the direct eight-hour flight overseas. I stayed awake the entire time because I was so anxious. When I arrived at the airport in Paris, everything was so confusing. I couldn't read or understand any of the signs. Even though I took a year of French in high school, nothing was recognizable. Being as inexperienced in international travel as I was, I didn't think to brush up on the language before my trip.

My cell phone plan didn't include international calls and texts, so I couldn't even call Ella for assistance or let my mom know I landed safely. After retrieving my luggage, I had to connect to Wi-Fi in order to utilize my cell phone. Ella and I didn't do a very good job of coordinating where we were going to meet, but she did give me basic instructions on how to get from the airport to the area where she lived.

I got on a train leaving the airport then transferred to a local subway system then got off somewhere in the middle of Paris. Emerging from the subway station, I was greeted by more signs I didn't understand. The fear of not having the slightest idea of where I was going was quickly overpowered by the mesmerizing feeling of being dropped into a storybook. From the store fronts to the cobblestone street, I was instantly transported to another land far different from anything I had ever seen before.

I wandered around, taking in the sights until I stumbled upon a small police station. I walked in, hoping one of the officers would recognize the directions I had scribbled on a piece of paper and would be able to tell me how to get there. Unfortunately, none of them were fluent in English. After using hand motions and talking very slowly for several minutes, I realized I was getting nowhere. Walking out of the station, I didn't think I was ever going to get to

Ella.

I tried to identify people who could possibly speak English to assist me when a young man approached me, making some sort of comment in French. I told him, "I'm sorry, but I don't speak French" to which he responded in English. Finally, there was hope!

I showed the young man my notes and he was nice enough to walk me to a train station and direct me where I needed to go. He even let me use his phone to call Ella to let her know I had arrived and to figure out where to meet. She told me to just stay put on the busy shopping street and she would come to me.

I waited near the entryway of a store with my large luggage, in the way of everyone trying to pass by, for about 30 minutes before Ella finally arrived. When I saw her, I sighed in relief that I wasn't going to be abandoned or abducted. It was nice to see a friendly face in a sea of unfamiliarity.

We spent the rest of the day exploring the city and getting settled into the one-bedroom apartment she shared with a roommate she found online before moving there. Her bed was situated where the living room used to be, which meant we would be sleeping together. She confided in me that her first few weeks there hadn't been smooth sailing but that she and her guy, Luc, were working on finding a balance in their relationship.

She couldn't wait to introduce me to the man who motivated her move across an ocean and had stolen her heart so quickly. She was also excited to introduce me to his best friend, Adrien. They had all been hanging out together, and she was confident he and I would hit it off.

The two of us took a taxi to the semi-professional

basketball game both guys were playing in. As we sat in the bleachers, she pointed out her boyfriend and then the guy she was trying to set me up with. The moment I laid eyes on him, I was sold.

Both guys looked like models shooting an ad for a sportswear company. Adrien was tall and athletic with creamy, caramel-colored skin. I guess birds of a feather really do flock together. Despite being ridiculously attractive, they were both two of the nicest people I had ever met. A total 180 from the way most attractive men in the states acted.

Adrien would meet with us daily to take us to exquisite French restaurants and show us around the city. Although I hesitated to indulge too much at first, eating crepes became my favorite thing to do. There were crepes available everywhere and it seemed like we had at least 3 a day.

For whatever reason, Luc was rarely available to spend time with us. Even though we should've been having the time of our lives in such an enchanting city, the fact that he was missing in action significantly brought Ella's mood down. Instead of cherishing every moment we had together to explore, the entire day, from morning to night, became about him.

She would wake up to argue with him over Facebook messenger then proceed to call him to continue the argument. While sightseeing, I would look over to find her crying. Then she would stop at random shops to ask if she could charge her phone because her battery had been depleted from texting him so much. While I was taking pictures of the Eiffel Tower and Notre Dame, she was lagging behind, focused on the screen of her phone.

Our time together was being overshadowed by her relationship. I travel across an ocean to spend the entire trip feeling like I was doing everything by myself. All of my memories were being tainted by her obsessing over why he couldn't make time for her. She had lost sight of what was important, which was that she had a friend there who came to visit her in the amazing city she was living in to share an once-in-a-lifetime experience.

I understood her being upset that he was constantly blowing her off, but no matter what I did to cheer her up, he was all she focused on. Eventually, I felt like I couldn't talk to her about anything other than Luc, so I started exploring the city by myself. I was tired of sitting around, waiting for her day to start after she recovered from their daily morning arguments.

Even though I didn't speak any French, I quickly learned how to navigate the subway system. After traveling to an area outside of the tourist focal points, I found a wonderful pub to have lunch at. The server was extremely nice and attentive; I think he felt bad after I told him why I was there alone.

He gave me the Wi-Fi code, supplied me with complementary drinks, and suggested amazing dishes for me to try. I ended up spending hours there meeting locals and finally having a lighthearted, good time with people who made me laugh. As I was heading out, Ella called me to ask where I was.

It was going to be an expensive phone call, but with the help of the many drinks I had, it was time to get my frustrations off my chest. I told her I didn't know exactly where I was, but that I needed space from her because her arguments with Luc and subsequent fall-outs were ruining my trip. After I said that, she started getting louder with me, so I got even louder. I ended up standing in the middle of the street, looking like 'one of those crazy Americans' screaming into the phone as Parisians walked, by staring at me.

I didn't travel so far to see her, just to feel like I was there alone. That wasn't the kind of trip I wanted to miss Thanksgiving with my family for. When I returned to her apartment, Ella was on the way out to start her first day at a new restaurant job. We didn't say a word to each other. After she left, I immediately called my mother with my credit card and flight information and begged her to find a way to change my return flight to an earlier date.

Since the tension was so high, I wanted to wait for Ella to get home from work to sit down with her and tell her I decided to leave early. I didn't take into consideration that when I booked my flight, I linked her email address in order to share the booking information with her, so when my mom changed my flight home, it also notified Ella.

As soon as she walked into the door of her apartment after getting off work, she blew up on me. Not only did she feel like the email was my way of informing her that I would be leaving the next day instead of four days later, but she couldn't believe I was leaving before her birthday. Nothing I said calmed her down, and she refused to see things from my perspective.

It was way too uncomfortable to stay with her in the same bed that night, so I packed up my things and asked Adrien if I could stay with him. After I explained the sudden need for somewhere else to stay, he was kind enough to pick me up and let me stay with him. If I had to spend my last night in Paris with anyone other than Ella, I wanted it to be him.

We walked into a large apartment in a swanky high-rise in the center of the city. He rented a room in the apartment, but he assured me his roommate was never home. We changed into pajamas and talked for a while about Ella and Luc and how hopefully things would blow over after I got back to the States. He didn't think they were good for each other, and he hoped their tumultuous courtship wasn't the cause for the end of our friendship.

Staring at Adrien's shirtless chiseled chest while we talked made me lose focus on anyone else but him. We began kissing while he played some of his favorite slow songs. I wanted to go further than kissing after discovering what he was working with in his sweatpants. Unfortunately, I was on the tail end of my period. It was only right that my period ruined the one good thing that could have come out of me having a fight with Ella and having to leave Paris early.

The next morning, Adrien drove me to the train station and encouraged me to reach out to Ella and try to smooth things over. He walked me to the entrance of the train station and kissed me like we were lovers parting ways before heading to work. He held both of his hands around my waist while looking into my eyes before one final kiss. If I had known our chemistry would be so strong, I would've kept my original return flight and stayed with him for those extra four days.

While on the train to the airport, I wrote Ella a very long, heartfelt email about why I left early and what went wrong. I repeatedly apologized about the way she found out that I changed my flight and that I wished the trip had turned out differently. I acknowledged that I could have exercised more patience and sympathy in the way I handled the situation, but after days of dealing with her emotional breakdowns and obsessive behavior, I decided it was best for me to remove myself from that environment.

She replied almost immediately with an angry response about how her relationship was none of my business and went on to tell me how ungrateful I was. To her, she had nothing to be sorry for. After all we had been through, I hoped she could at least respect my decision and admit she could've handled things differently as well.

Since so many years had passed, my hope was that time

had healed whatever wounds were created during my trip to Paris. When I searched for her name on Facebook, nothing came up. I thought that maybe she had blocked me, but nothing came up when my mom searched either. I didn't have her phone number and she was no longer in any of my contact list. Nothing resulted from an internet search of her, either.

The only person we had in common was Adrien, so I reached out to him on Facebook in the hopes he had some sort of contact information for her. He sent me a message back saying he hadn't seen or heard from her in over two years. His only suggestion was to add her on Skype and provided me with her new handle.

After looking her up, I realized there was already a pending contact request she never approved. Even though I re-sent my contact request, she never accepted. By chance, my mom saw a post from her under a different name on Facebook where she stated she was resurfacing after deleting her account and provided her Instagram handle and email address so people could stay in touch.

Maybe it was fate that while I was looking for her, she posted that message. I wrote her a short and sweet email about how I missed her and that I hoped we could rebuild our friendship. I saw on Instagram that she was living in New York, and since I would frequently take the trips there, I hoped that we could meet for coffee.

She never responded. I did everything possible to reach out to her in order to repair our relationships but I couldn't force my friendship on anyone. The only thing I could do was hope that one day our paths would cross again.

My reconciling record wasn't looking great. I had one strike but that didn't deter from reaching out to the next person, Elijah. Working through what I had done wrong in my relationship with Colin helped me realize how many mistakes I made with Elijah. At the time, I thought he was insensitive and mean. In reality, I had been spoiled, impatient, unreasonable, and overzealous.

My twenties were my time to grow and learn more about myself and improve how I dealt with other people. I learned to compromise and communicate better. That growth helped make me a better friend, girlfriend, and overall person. Even when someone else couldn't admit when they had done something wrong, I had to learn to forgive and let go of any resentment or anger.

I sent Elijah an icebreaker on Facebook, asking if he remembered the portrait I drew of him when I landed in California. He responded almost immediately with, "Sort of. How have you been?" Clearly, that drawing still meant nothing to him. He probably threw it away as soon as I left, but I didn't want to start the conversation on a sour note so I moved on.

Over the next couple of days, we continuously sent messages back and forth as if no time had passed. Previously, I had done a full removal of him from my electronic life, so I asked his permission to add him back to my Skype contacts. He told me that was a great idea.

One night, he asked me when we would be able to video chat. I told him no time like the present and arranged the lighting in my living room, fixed my hair, and put on minimal makeup to create the illusion that I had done nothing to get ready for it. The first words out of his mouth were, "You still look as beautiful as ever."

From that night on, we were in constant communication. There were times when he would forgo sleep to stay up and video chat with me for four or five hours at a time. We discussed everything from our future aspirations to our views on the current state of the black community, and then we covered relationships we had been in since we last spoke. I told him about my relationship with Colin and why it ended. He complained about still being single and wanting to shift his priorities from work to family.

He said, "The only reason I would move back to the States would be to settle down." So I asked him, "How do you expect to find a significant other from Afghanistan?" He didn't believe in online dating and he was adamant about settling down with a black woman, which meant he wasn't going to find love in the Middle East unless they worked together.

In my mind, the possibility of the two of us being together romantically had passed, so I would engage him in order to be a friendly sounding board. I tried to help him figure out ways to meet eligible women and assist him with the courting process when he did meet someone.

Even if it wasn't with me, I felt like he was deserving of a great love. He had spent so many years working so far away from home in order to support his family and build a substantial life for himself that it was time for him to start living his own life.

After a few weeks our video chats turned from friendly to flirty. He started asking me if I still took sexy photos in lingerie, like the ones I sent to him while we first met. I was mortified. I hoped that he didn't still have those photos because I can't imagine I looked very sexy. I told him there was no reason for me to take those kinds of photos because I had no one to send them to. He told me I could send some to him.

In order for me to go down that path, he needed to send me

something first, so he sent me a shirtless photo with his pants barely visible in the shot. When I opened the image I blushed. Looking at his half-naked body on my computer screen made me warm, among other things. I didn't return the favor right away, but with every video chat I had less and less clothes on.

The conversations then went from sexy to serious. He began asking me if I wanted kids, if I would be willing to relocate, and what I wanted my life to look like when I settled down. While sharing some of our conversations with Elaine and Laurel from work, they began to speculate about me being someone he could come back to the States for.

I couldn't allow myself to think like that. I tried my hardest not to do what I did the first time, take every kind word or sweet gesture and turn them into reassurances. Even though, unlike when we met 4 years ago, he was a lot more forthcoming about his feelings and what he wanted.

During those chats, we had some very serious conversations about what went wrong between us the first time. We gave each other the opportunity to address any issues or misunderstandings we had been holding on to. The last time we stopped speaking was because of a comment he made over Facebook.

During one of the times Colin and I had split up, Elijah and I would talk briefly about how the other was doing. He asked how I was doing and I mentioned to him that I was trying to lose weight in order to get my self-confidence back. He replied, "You have some areas you could work on if you are trying to achieve the perfect body", which I took as an insult that deeply hurt my feelings. Afterwards, I shared what he said in an anonymous status that resulted in all of the commenters bashing him over such an insensitive response.

After I made our conversation public (without actually naming him as the offender), he didn't feel comfortable responding and we stopped talking for a year. He clarified that his statement was meant to be sarcastic and that he thought I looked great the way I was. He went on to tell me how I couldn't get any more beautiful, inside or out. There were even times where he bragged to his coworkers about me, showing off my pictures and telling them I was his model friend.

He told me how smart, funny, and kind he thought I was, how I had so much to offer, and that I deserved someone who would appreciate me. I couldn't believe how he was showering me with compliments. In the past, I couldn't remember him uttering anything nice or supportive.

Maybe this was a new Elijah. Or maybe my memories were too hard on him. I wanted to explore the kind, open, and honest version of him before he turned back into a pumpkin. I couldn't help but think that our time apart was simply grooming us to come back to each other at the right time. Maybe the period at the end of our love story was really just...

During one of our video chats, he mentioned that he was coming back to the States within the next few weeks for leave. What perfect timing, I thought to myself. I asked if I would be able to see him and he was surprised. His short time back was going to be pretty full, but he said he would make time to see me.

He told me about the several stops he had planned, including Houston, Atlanta, Puerto Rico, and of course Wisconsin to spend time with his family. His purpose for going to Puerto Rico was for vacation, but he told me the rest were to look at investment properties. The two weeks he had for leave seemed jam-packed, but I was confident we could make time for each other.

My hope was that when we saw each other, it would solidify the feelings that hadn't gone away after all of those years, no matter how hard I tried. There were only a handful of people who knew about the entirety of our saga. The girls at work I confided in were so excited for us to reunite because no matter what guys I dated over the last 4 years, they always hoped he and I would end up together.

No matter how long we went without speaking, I always felt like my heart belonged to him. We would always pick back up as we were before we stopped speaking, no matter the reason. The same feelings would flood back. With every rekindling they grew stronger.

The more he shared his thoughts and experiences with me, the more I wanted to know. During the times we would talk about our views on the world and what we wanted out of life, it sounded as if he was speaking my thoughts before I could get them out. We had such different life experiences, but ultimately we wanted the same things.

My days were that much brighter with him in them. Every time I would get an alert on my phone, I hoped it was him. I downloaded every app I could in order to stay in touch with him. There wasn't a time when he would message me and I didn't smile. With the 8 hour time difference, I would stay up late to talk to him before he went to work, and before he went to bed we would talk before I had to go to work.

All of that changed when he boarded a plane to come back to the States. What happened next was like déjà vu from the time he left Virginia years ago. On Facebook, I could see him check in at various airports but I didn't hear from him. I did my best not revert back to my old ways and obsessively check my phone. I wanted to play it cool and give him space.

While he was in Wisconsin, we did video chat one time, but during the rest of his time in the States, there wasn't much communication. Before his trip I was so excited and hopeful. Then I ended up being confused and disappointed. I went from floating on a cloud to feeling like someone put a 'kick me' sign on my back.

One day, a bartender from work started talking to me about her relationship and asked about what was going on in my love life. I gave her an abbreviated version of my history with Elijah and how he had been acting as of late. She went on to tell me about the on-and-off boyfriend she dated for over seven years after high school.

After one bad break-up, she spent every night praying about whether he was the right one for her. She asked over and over for God to give her a sign. She didn't want to give up on someone she had been with for so long, but she also didn't want to waste any more time on a guy who wasn't right for her.

A month later, he asked to get back together. They were fine for a while, but then one night during an argument he struck her in the face. She said, "That was my sign". He didn't come back into her life for them to stay together. He came back to give her the definitive answer that she needed to finally let him go.

I listened very carefully to her story. I completely understood the lesson she was trying to share with me. But in my heart, I believed Elijah came back into my life to stay. I assured her that he was just busy traveling and that I was confident that I would see him before he left to go back to Afghanistan. The assurance was more for me than her.

Over the next week my spirits began to drop significantly. His time was coming to an end and still no word from him. I had to throw in the towel. Seeing how we had just reconnected and his trip was already planned I couldn't be upset with him about not being able to see each other. Communication on the other hand was well within his abilities.

I should've just licked my wounds and left it alone but I felt like I needed to let him know how disappointed I was. I sent him a text that said, "I'm not sure what happened to you, but if you didn't want to keep in touch, you could've let me know. If I don't hear from you, I wish you the best of luck." I didn't curse him out or throw stones. I didn't want to blow up before I knew the reason behind his disappearance.

A few hours later, he texted me back, "No, no, that's not the case. I've just been very busy. Things haven't been going as planned." He went on to tell me that he had planned too many things in too little time and it was overall a rough trip. As relieved as I was to hear from him, I needed to have a real conversation, not just a few texts over a series of hours. He said he would call me when he was free.

As I walked into the entrance of Harry's while on break, my phone rang. My heart raced as I answered it. From the moment I picked up the phone, something felt off. The conversation felt forced, which made the phone call extremely uncomfortable. Even though he was answering all of my questions, I could tell he was hiding something.

I asked about how his vacation had been so far and he told me his luggage had been lost early on, including his laptop, which he needed for every stop of his trip. I asked him specifically how Puerto Rico was since he had just returned, but his answers were odd. He went on to tell me about all of the activities he participated in, but never mentioned anyone else.

Usually, when someone recaps a vacation, the people they went with are brought up at some point. He tried to move on to another subject, but I just couldn't let that go so I asked him, "Who did you go to Puerto Rico with?" After a long pause, he said his best friend Maggie, who he mentioned before that she was going, but then he mentioned two other women he claimed to know from working in Afghanistan.

That was an odd dynamic to me, one man and three women on a vacation together. So I said, "It was just you and a bunch of women?" To which he snapped, "It wasn't a bunch!" I responded with a hesitant "Okay" and tried to move past the uneasy feeling building in my gut.

When I asked where he was at the time, he said, "Chicago." I thought to myself, he never mentioned going to Chicago before. I asked him, "Are you by yourself?" to which he responded, "Right now?" The red flags were flying at me nonstop. I couldn't put my finger on what was going on with him, but throughout the entire conversation he was elusive and hesitant.

When I encouraged him to go on, he confirmed that he was in a car by himself. I needed a minute to gather my thoughts, so I told him I would call him later and hurriedly got off the phone. I immediately texted Laurel and gave her a play-by-play of the conversation. When I was done, she asked me, "Do you think he has a girlfriend?"

The thought never crossed my mind. For the previous few weeks we had been talking, we had discussed every detail about what had been going on in our lives. I asked him repeatedly about whether or not he was dating anyone. Every time, he told me there was no one.

When I called him later that night, there was no answer. I gave it a day. When he didn't call back, I called again the following night. No answer.

Two days later, I received a message that he had been traveling back to Afghanistan so he couldn't answer my calls. I didn't respond because everything we had built before his trip to the States had crumbled and I had no idea why. I couldn't even formulate into words how confused about it I was.

I clicked on Elijah's Facebook page to see if I could piece together what really went on during his vacation. He never really posted a lot of pictures, but many times people would tag him in posts. As I scrolled down his news feed, a female I had never seen on his page before simply posted a heart emoji on his wall.

As a female, I knew exactly what that girl was doing. In order to mark one's territory on a guy's social media, most women don't write long, drawn-out posts; they strategically make their comments short and sweet to let other women know that she's a part of the guy's life. Of course I clicked on her page to investigate further.

She had recently changed her background photo to a beautiful sunset on the beach. In the comments, someone asked, "Where did you go?" Underneath, she responded, "Puerto Rico". The same place Elijah vacationed at alongside two unidentified females. A tiny explosion went off in my head as I read those words.

When I looked at her information, it said she worked for the government and was located in Chicago. Where Elijah was the last time I talked to him. That time, a slightly bigger bomb went off.

Then I kept scrolling to discover that days before she had changed her relationship status to "In a relationship with..." Wait for it..."Elijah Baker". Soul-shattering explosion.

The reason I had been wearing a dunce hat all of that time had been revealed. The pieces of the puzzle he refused to give me, I'd found on my own. All it took was a heart emoji.

I was upset but I didn't cry. The fact that he was leading me on after all of that time meant that I never really meant anything to him in the first place. I didn't want an explanation. I didn't want closure. I didn't want to curse him out. I just wanted to be free from the delusion that he was the man I was meant to spend the rest of my life with.

He obviously had made his choice, and it wasn't me. The entire time he and I were having late-night video chats, he was making travel plans with his girlfriend. His deception made it much easier for me to let go. I had made a fool of myself long enough by boasting about him to my friends and holding out hope that after 4 years things would end any differently.

After a few days of silence, he sent me a message on Skype like we would fall back into old habits. It seemed he didn't know that I had followed the breadcrumbs his girlfriend had left on his timeline. I sat at my computer for a few minutes, typing sentence after sentence and then deleting it.

Finally, I sent him a message:

You have been a mirage that I have tried to turn into something real for the past 4 years. I've raved about how being with you was magical and how captivating you were. Now, I realize you will never exist in my life as something real. All this time, I've been hoping that my moment would come, the stars would align, and we would live a life filled with love together. Instead, I'm left with nothing but a man I built up in my mind, who isn't the man you've turned out to be. Maybe I saw things differently than what they really were or maybe I ignored all of the warning signs, but that is solely my burden to bear. I have to move on from the fairy tale I've been hoping for in order to find something real.

I had to admit to myself that the feelings I had been holding onto and trying to recreate from our first two weeks together were never going to be reciprocated. It would've been easy to bash him for leading me on by periodically giving me morsels of hope, but I had to admit my part in the cycle. He couldn't keep me on the line if I didn't keep coming back.

This definitely wasn't a happy ending. No matter what I did or said, I couldn't make a relationship between us work if that wasn't what he wanted. It was time to let go of the hope that one day he would feel the feelings I had felt for him from the moment he told me we should get married on the first night we met.

As turning 30th crept closer, I started to think about what I wanted out of life. I still wanted to fall in love and get married and have babies, but what if that never happened? Was I supposed to sit around waiting for a man in order for the rest of my life to start?

There was no way for me to say with full confidence that my soulmate was out there. Maybe I had already met him and our window of opportunity had passed us by. If we had yet to meet, there was no guarantee we would find each other. There were so many guys all over the world; how was I to know that out of all the women available, there was one man waiting just for me? That unknown made me uneasy.

The idea of going out on more dead-end dates or spending

nights out at a bar or club in order to meet men became less attractive the older I got. My dating pool was getting smaller and the men available were getting less appealing. In my early twenties, I felt like I had all the time in the world to settle down, dating guys but never taking them too seriously. I was picky, flippant, and careless. Dating was no longer a sprint, it was a marathon.

As hard as I tried to not let being single bring me down, I still felt like there was a checklist of things I was supposed to achieve by 30, and having a man was one box I couldn't check as completed yet. The pressure was mainly in my head, but society didn't help any.

Every time someone said to me, "There's no way you're single" and I replied that, in fact, I was, their question was followed by the 'You must be crazy' look. I wanted to wither away to avoid their judgmental gaze. Maybe I was crazy. Maybe I was cursed. Maybe my husband was around the next corner. Or maybe I was meant to be alone.

Whatever the reason was for being single for most of my adult life, I didn't want that to define me. Being alone was better than being in an unhappy and unfilled relationship. Which I tried to remind myself of every time I laid in bed at night alone.

For so long, I had sacrificed so much of myself to hold onto one-sided relationships, only to end up heartbroken. Unless a man was willing to treasure my heart and make me feel special every day then being single wasn't a consolation prize, it meant more time to cherish myself. I needed to stay focused on my mental and physical well-being, learn to love myself more each day, and make decisions based on what made me happy before thinking of anyone else.

Whether or not love and marriage would be a part of my future, it didn't mean I had to sacrifice happiness, joy, and invaluable experiences. Even though I had been fed images of what my life was supposed to look like through movies and television, my happy ending was what I made it.

My worth wasn't going to be defined by whether or not I had a man. There were so many accomplishments I had and would continue to achieve, and they had nothing to do with my relationship status. Until I met the man who was going to fulfill me, I would work towards having a full life by myself. No more settling for crumbs.

About the Author

Serita Braxton is a former government contract employee who left her day job for an exciting and unpredictable position as a cocktail server at a prestigious and trendy rooftop bar based in Washington, DC. She put on hold her creative aspirations to complete college and pursue a career. After years of postponement, she was able to craft and publish her first novel, her memoir *More Than Crumbs*.